D0516015

# The
# Connecticut Colony

**by Dennis Brindell Fradin**

Consultant: Alesandra M. Schmidt
The Connecticut Historical Society
Hartford, Connecticut

 CHILDRENS PRESS®
CHICAGO

**Dedication**

For Helen Handler, With Love

**Library of Congress Cataloging-in-Publication Data**

Fradin, Dennis B.
    The Connecticut Colony / by Dennis B. Fradin.
      p.  cm.
    Summary: Surveys the history of the colony of Connecticut from its early
days up through the American Revolution. Includes biographical sketches of
prominent individuals.
    ISBN 0-516-00393-3
    1. Connecticut—History—Colonial period, ca. 1600-1775—Juvenile
literature. 2. Connecticut—History—Colonial period, ca. 1600-1775—
Biography—Juvenile literature. 3. Connecticut—History—Revolution, 1775-
1783—Juvenile literature. 4. Connecticut—History—Revolution, 1775-1783—
Biography—Juvenile literature. 5. Connecticut—Biography—Juvenile
literature. [1. Connecticut—History—Colonial period, ca. 1600-1775.
2. Connecticut—History—Revolution, 1775-1783.] I. Title.
F97.F73   1990
974.6'02—dc20                                      89-29205
                                                        CIP
                                                         AC

# Table of Contents

Windsor Locks on the Connecticut River.

## COLONIAL AMERICA

Maine
(Part of
Massachusetts)

New Hampshire

New
York

Massachusetts

Rhode Island

Connecticut

Pennsylvania

New Jersey

Delaware

Virginia

Maryland

APPALACHIAN MOUNTAINS

North Carolina

South
Carolina

ATLANTIC
OCEAN

Georgia

Connecticut was one of the thirteen American colonies that England founded or took over along the East Coast of what is now the United States. In the order that they were first permanently settled, the Thirteen Colonies were Virginia (1607), Massachusetts (1620), New Hampshire (1623), New York (1624), Connecticut (1633), Maryland (1634), Rhode Island (1636), Delaware (1638), Pennsylvania (1643), North Carolina (about 1653), New Jersey (1660), South Carolina (1670), and Georgia (1733).

# Chapter I

## A Connecticut Overview

*Yankee Doodle went to town,*
*Riding on a pony,*
*Stuck a feather in his hat,*
*And called it macaroni.*

> *From "Yankee Doodle," Connecticut's state song*

Connecticut is one of the six New England states, which are located in the northeastern corner of the United States. The other five New England states are Maine, Massachusetts, New Hampshire, Rhode Island, and Vermont. Connecticut's neighboring states are Massachusetts to the north, Rhode Island to the east, and New York to the west. The arm of the Atlantic Ocean called Long Island Sound splashes against Connecticut's southern shore.

Of the fifty states, only Rhode Island and Delaware are smaller than Connecticut. But despite its small size, Connecticut has one of the richest histories of the fifty states.

Connecticut was settled in the 1630s by English people from Massachusetts, many of whom were seeking greater freedom of religion. Because religion meant so much to the Connecticut colonists, they built a society in which the Bible and the churches were very important. The Connecticut colonists also valued self-rule. Connecticut and Rhode Island had more control over their own affairs than any of the other colonies.

Connecticut's self-government was protected by a document called a charter that the king of England granted in 1662. The most famous event in the Connecticut Colony's history took place in 1687, when an English official tried to seize the charter and take away many of the colony's privileges. Connecticut people hid their charter— reportedly in an oak tree in Hartford later called the Charter Oak. Connecticut soon returned to its large degree of self-rule. Its colonists quietly went about their business with little trouble from England for almost 100 years after that.

The Connecticut colonists earned a reputation for being very conservative—meaning that they liked to stick to ways that had worked in the past. Connecticut lawmakers commonly served twenty-five years or more in the same position, because the voters were very loyal to those who did a good

The Charter Oak was destroyed by a windstorm in 1856.

job. Also, unlike several other colonies, Connecticut had no large cities and very poor roads. Rather than going to a city to buy clothing, household utensils, and farm tools, people stayed on their farms and made these things themselves. Because its people were content to keep to the old ways and to stay at home, Connecticut was nicknamed the Land of Steady Habits in colonial times. This is still one of Connecticut's nicknames today.

Starting in the 1760s, the English government tried to make the Americans pay taxes on many items ranging from legal papers to tea. The Thirteen Colonies then rebelled against English rule. They fought and won the Revolutionary War (1775–1783) to break free of England and become the United States of America.

Although no major Revolutionary War battles were fought there, Connecticut sent many thousands of men and a large amount of supplies to George Washington's Continental Army. Because of Connecticut's great contributions, George Washington nicknamed it the Provisions State. Connecticut Governor Jonathan Trumbull, who played a key role in the American effort, was nicknamed Brother Jonathan by George Washington. Brother Jonathan was a nickname for the United States in its early years, just as Uncle Sam is a nickname for the U. S. government today.

Connecticut also produced one of the greatest patriots in American history during the Revolutionary War. He was Captain Nathan Hale, a former schoolteacher, who was captured by the British while on a spying mission. Just before he was hanged, Nathan Hale said the famous words, "I only regret that I have but one life to lose for my country."

Nathan Hale

A few years after separating from England, the United States made a set of national laws called the U. S. Constitution. The leaders who created the Constitution could not agree on certain matters. Roger Sherman of Connecticut helped solve a big dispute. Connecticut's main nickname, the Constitution State, may have resulted from

Sherman's contribution to the U. S. Constitution. However, some historians think the nickname was inspired by Connecticut's Fundamental Orders, a set of laws that were approved in 1639 and that have been called the first written constitution in the English-speaking world.

Perhaps because of their tradition of making the things they needed, Connecticut people were responsible for many inventions and manufacturing breakthroughs during the 1800s. In 1808, Eli Terry of the Hartford area became the first person to manufacture clocks in large numbers. In the 1830s, Samuel Colt of Hartford invented the repeating pistol. In 1839, Charles Goodyear of Naugatuck discovered a process called vulcanization that made rubber stronger. In 1848, Linus Yale of Stamford invented the first modern lock. During the 1800s, Connecticut people created many other inventions ranging from the first coin-operated telephone to the electric streetcar.

Samuel Colt

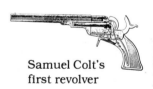

Samuel Colt's first revolver

These inventions helped Connecticut change from a farming to a manufacturing state. During the 1800s, factories making such items as clocks, sewing machines, guns, locks, and rubber goods were established in Connecticut. Also during that century, the city of Hartford (which in 1875 became Connecticut's only capital) became known

Hartford, Connecticut, in the 1800s

as a center for the insurance business. By 1900, manufacturing was more important than farming in Connecticut, and Hartford was a leading city in the insurance industry.

Manufacturing is now by far the main way of earning a living in Connecticut. Factories turn out such products as jet engines, submarines, machine tools, silverware, clocks, and chemicals. Connecticut is also home to thousands of people who work in New York City, which is just a few miles from Connecticut's southwestern corner.

For a small state, Connecticut has produced a remarkable number of famous people. One of the state's most famous "daughters" was the author

Harriet Beecher Stowe (1811–1896), who was born in Litchfield. She wrote *Uncle Tom's Cabin* (published 1851–1852), a novel that helped convince many people that slavery was evil.

Noah Webster (1758–1843) was one of Connecticut's most famous "sons." Born in West Hartford, Webster became a teacher and an author who wrote a spelling book, a grammar book, and a reader for children. Later in life he compiled his famous *Webster's Dictionary*, which is still being revised and printed.

Harriet Beecher Stowe

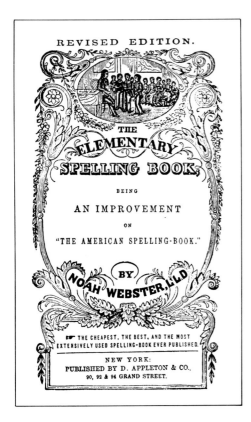

An 1890 edition of Noah Webster's spelling book (left). The title page of Harriet Beecher Stowe's *Uncle Tom's Cabin* (below)

Noah Webster

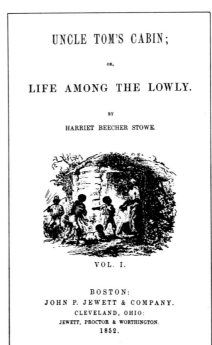

Phineas T. Barnum

Another Connecticut man, P. T. Barnum (1810–1891) of Bethel, ran a very famous circus called The Greatest Show on Earth. Asaph Hall (1829–1907) of Goshen was an astronomer who discovered the two little moons of Mars in 1877. John Fitch (1743–1798) of the Hartford area invented one of the first steamboats. Connecticut was also home to a number of famous colonial Americans.

Besides all its fascinating history and people, Connecticut is very lovely. Thousands of years ago, the land was covered by glaciers. When these ice sheets melted, they left hundreds of little lakes across Connecticut. The Constitution State also has many waterfalls on its numerous rivers, which include the Connecticut, the Housatonic, and the Thames. And it has beaches and islands along its southern coast, and low mountains in the northwest.

In addition, nearly two-thirds of Connecticut is covered by forests, making it one of America's more wooded states. Hundreds of years ago, when Indians were the only people there, Connecticut was an incredibly beautiful region that was almost completely wooded. Since the Indians were there first, it is with them that we begin our story of the Connecticut Colony.

The wooded banks of the Housatonic River are noted for their scenic beauty.

The Indians used birch bark to construct homes and canoes.

# Chapter II

# The Indians of Connecticut

*The Indians, at their [the colonists'] first settlement, performed many acts of kindness towards them. They instructed them in the manner of planting and dressing the Indian corn. They carried them upon their backs, through rivers and waters. . . . They gave them much useful information respecting the country, and when the English or their children were lost in the woods, and were in danger of perishing with hunger or cold, they conducted them to their wigwams, fed them, and restored them to their families and parents.*

From A Complete History of Connecticut, *by Benjamin Trumbull (1818)*

Before colonists came to Connecticut, Indians lived there. They were members of the Algonquian family of tribes. Some of the larger tribes were the Pequot, the Niantic, the Saukiog, the Tunxis, and the Quinnipiac. There were also a number of other tribes, some with as few as fifty members. A rather small tribe called the Podunk had a village called Podunk near what is now Hartford. To this day, people sometimes refer to a small town as a Podunk.

Connecticut's Indians lived in villages built mainly along the seacoast and the rivers. To build a home, the Indians first cut down a large number of young trees. They planted the thin tree trunks firmly in the ground as a framework for the house. Then they covered the framework with branches, bark, and reeds to make the walls and ceiling. Some of these houses were reportedly 100 feet long by 30 feet wide. For protection, some villages were surrounded by wooden fences.

The Indians grew much of their food. They used hoes made of large shells attached to wooden handles to till their fields. Often the whole village would work together and prepare the field for planting. The women and children grew the corn and beans. The only crop the men grew was tobacco, which was smoked during religious ceremonies.

The Connecticut Indians also hunted and fished. In long-ago times, Connecticut was teeming with wild turkeys, quail, partridges, pigeons, ducks, deer, bears, and moose. The men hunted these animals with bows and arrows, traps, and clubs. Generally a man went out alone to hunt for his family. But now and then dozens of men went on long hunting trips, sometimes taking along their wives and children.

The men fished from canoes, which they paddled along the region's many rivers and out on Long Island Sound. They caught sturgeon and other fish with hooks, spears, and nets. At times children were given little spears and allowed to come along on these fishing trips. The children and the women also helped gather oysters, clams, and lobsters.

The women cooked the food in pots made of baked clay. One of the Indians' favorite dishes was succotash—a blend of beans and corn that was sometimes flavored with fish. Their other foods included cornmeal cakes and vegetable and meat stews. Special treats were the strawberries, blackberries, walnuts, and chestnuts that were gathered at different seasons.

Indian basket

Workbag made by an Indian

The forest and its animals provided all the items the Indians used in their daily lives. They cut knots off hardwood trees and made them into bowls. They made baskets out of the long grass they found near marshes, and water pails out of birch bark. Various plants yielded medicines. The skins of deer, bears, wolves, foxes, and wildcats were made into clothes and blankets.

The people who lived across the Atlantic Ocean in Europe tended to have large families—often ten children or more. Indian parents tended to have small families, which was a main reason why fewer than 10,000 Indians lived in Connecticut in the early 1600s.

What the Indian family lacked in size, it made up for in love. Parents were very affectionate toward their children. It was rare for a parent to strike a child. Instead, parents tried to help children understand why things should be done in certain ways. Indian children did not go to school. They learned how to take their place in the adult world by working alongside their elders.

When a young male Indian decided that he wanted to marry a young woman, he gave her presents of *wampum*. These were pretty shell beads that the Indians made into belts. If the

White and purple wampum

woman accepted the young man's wampum, it meant that she agreed to marry him. Then the chief of the tribe, called the *sachem*, came to the couple and joined their hands together. This made them husband and wife. They then built a home and began to cultivate their own fields.

The Indians were a very religious people. But unlike the Europeans, who worshiped one God, the Indians believed in many gods. Their main god was known to the various tribes by such names as Kiehtan, Woonand, and Cautantowit. He was said to live far off to the southwest, in the region of the warm winds. The Indians believed that, when they died, they would go to Kiehtan's home in the southwest. Kiehtan opened his door to the good souls, who then lived with him forever in happiness. The evil souls were turned away. They wandered about forever, causing a great deal of mischief on earth.

The Indians feared an evil god, Hobbamocko, who caused disease and bad luck. They also had dozens of gods associated with the stars, the wind, the rivers, fire, and other aspects of nature. And there was a god named Muckachuckwand who was the special protector of children.

To please their good gods, and to keep Hobbamocko from harming them, the Indians held religious festivals throughout the year. They danced at these festivals to make the gods happy. Sometimes they sacrificed animals. They also smoked tobacco, because the gods were thought to love its smell.

Certain places were believed to be holy to the gods. One such place in Connecticut was Mount Tom, in what is now the southeastern part of the state. Strange noises could be heard at Mount Tom, possibly due to the shifting of underground rocks. The Indians thought that the rumblings were the voices of the kind god Kiehtan and the evil god Hobbamocko.

For the most part, the various tribes got along well with each other. Sachems were expected to welcome travelers and ambassadors from other tribes into their homes. There were also occasions when tribes from different regions visited each other. The inland tribes would paddle downstream to feast on oysters and lobsters with the seacoast tribes. Then the seacoast tribes would paddle upriver to visit the inland people. There were language differences between the tribes, but they were minor and the people could understand one another.

Although they usually settled their disputes peacefully, occasionally the tribes made war on each other. Once war was declared, the Indians were all-out fighters. They made predawn attacks in which they killed and scalped some of their enemies. However, prisoners who were not killed were often adopted by the victors. A family who wanted another child would raise an enemy child as their own.

Many Indians welcomed the English colonists who began arriving in Connecticut in the 1630s. The colonists, however, took advantage of the Native Americans in land deals and even fought some of them. Thousands of Indians were killed or pushed out of their homes, and some Connecticut tribes disappeared completely. Today, only about 8,000 Indians live in Connecticut, less than half of them related to the region's original tribes.

This French map of New England shows the Connecticut Colony along the Connecticut River

Painting showing settlers arriving at the site of Hartford, Connecticut, in 1636.

# Chapter III

# Exploration and First Colonists

*The country abounded with a great variety of wild fruit. In the groves were walnuts, chestnuts, butternuts, hazelnuts, and acorns in great abundance. Wild cherries, currants, and plums were natural productions. In the low lands, on the banks of the rivers . . . was a variety . . . of grapes. The country also abounded with . . . strawberries, blackberries of various kinds, raspberries, dewberries, whortleberries, bilberries, blueberries, and mulberries. Cranberries also grew plenteously in the meadows. . . .*

> *Description of some of Connecticut's plant life when the first Europeans arrived. From Benjamin Trumbull's* A Complete History of Connecticut *(1818)*

## THE DUTCH CAME FIRST

The area that became the Connecticut Colony was located about 500 miles northeast of the Virginia Colony. Virginia, the first of England's thirteen American colonies, was founded in 1607, when English people began building the settlement of Jamestown.

But England was not the only country that was interested in the East Coast of what is now the

United States. France, Spain, Sweden, and The Netherlands also had their eyes on the region. In fact, a Dutchman (a man from The Netherlands) named Adriaen Block was the first known European to explore present-day Connecticut. Block did not cross the Atlantic Ocean to explore Connecticut. Instead, his trip to Connecticut was the result of a disaster that befell him in nearby New York.

Block and his men came to what is now New York state in a small ship named the *Tiger* in 1613. They traded for furs with the Indians along the Hudson River, then anchored the *Tiger* off what is now New York City. Somehow the *Tiger* caught fire and was destroyed, but Block and his crew swam to Manhattan Island. Friendly Indians helped the Dutchmen build cabins where they passed the winter, thus becoming the first known Europeans to live in what is now New York City.

When spring of 1614 arrived, Block and his men cut down trees on Manhattan Island. They used the timber to build a ship called the *Onrust* (a Dutch word meaning *Restless*). Captain Block knew that the *Onrust* was too small to cross the Atlantic Ocean, so he decided to explore nearby regions with it. This is how he happened to explore Connecticut.

Captain Adriaen Block and his men building the *Onrust*.

Captain Block sailed the *Onrust* through Long Island Sound to Connecticut's southern coast. He stopped for a short time at the mouth of the Housatonic River, then continued to the mouth of what the Indians called *Quinnehtukqut*, or Long River. English colonists later kept this Indian name for the river and also gave it to the colony— only they changed the spelling to *Connecticut*.

The Indians brought furs to trade with the Europeans.

Captain Block and his men stopped on the Connecticut River at the spot where Hartford now stands. The Saukiog Indian tribe had a town there, also called Saukiog. The Dutchmen spent two weeks with the friendly Indians at Saukiog, trading with them for furs.

Continuing up the river, Block reached what is now northern Connecticut before finding that he could no longer navigate the river. He then retraced his route south into Long Island Sound and went on to explore Rhode Island. Block and his crew finally met a larger ship that brought them home to The Netherlands.

Based on explorations by Adriaen Block, Henry Hudson, and others, The Netherlands claimed parts of what are now New York, New Jersey, Connecticut, and Delaware. They named this region New Netherland. The Dutch founded what is now New York City in 1625 along with a lot of other colonization in what is now New York state. They paid little attention to Connecticut, however.

A few Dutch traders did visit Connecticut during the next few years. They traded trinkets to the Indians for furs, which were made into clothes and hats back in Europe. In 1633, the Dutch built a small combination fort and trading post where Hartford now stands. Called the House of Hope, it was manned by a few Dutch soldiers and traders. But the Dutch did not build towns in Connecticut or send settlers there.

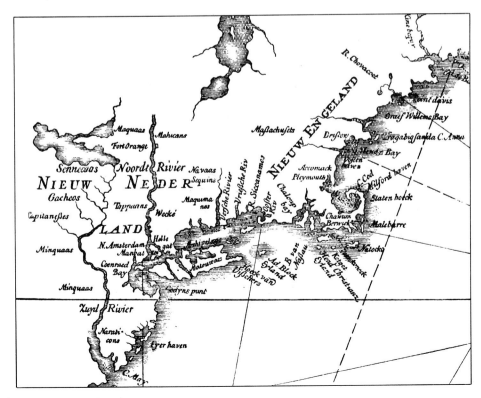

A Dutch map, drawn in 1630, shows New Netherland and New England.

## ENGLISH PEOPLE BECOME INTERESTED IN CONNECTICUT

About the time that the Dutch were building the House of Hope, English people were becoming interested in Connecticut. To understand why, it helps to understand conditions in England and in Massachusetts at that time.

Back in the early 1600s, people in England could not worship as they pleased. People who quit the Church of England (the country's official religion) could lose their jobs and be imprisoned. Even people who criticized the Church of England could be punished.

Because they felt that the Church of England had abandoned Biblical ideas, many thousands of English people criticized or quit the church despite the risks. Those who worked to improve the church without leaving it were called Puritans. This name came from their desire to purify the church—to make it better. A smaller number of people, called Separatists, quit the Church of England and formed their own congregations. In order to escape discovery, the Separatists sometimes worshiped in barns and in people's homes. But thousands of Separatists and Puritans who were identified by the king lost their jobs and property. Some were jailed.

Massachusetts was founded by English people who hoped to escape religious persecution in England. In 1620, the Separatist group known as the Pilgrims founded Plymouth in what became the Massachusetts Colony. In 1630, a larger group of Puritans founded Boston in the Massachusetts Colony. Massachusetts was the second of England's thirteen American colonies, after Virginia.

Puritans

The Massachusetts colonists had left England because of religious persecution. Yet once in the new country, they in turn persecuted people who disagreed with them on religious matters. This was especially true around Boston, where the Puritans expelled a number of people who held unpopular religious views. There were also many people who left Massachusetts of their own free will. Some of the people who left Massachusetts settled other colonies.

In 1636, Roger Williams had to leave Massachusetts because of his religious beliefs. That year he founded Providence, the first permanent town in the Rhode Island Colony. In 1638, the year she was expelled from the church, Anne Hutchinson left Massachusetts, and helped to found Portsmouth, the second permanent town in Rhode Island. Others who fled Massachusetts because of

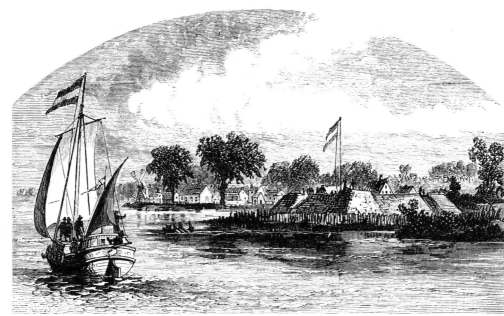

A fortified trading post in Connecticut

religious bigotry were among the early settlers of Maine (then part of Massachusetts) and New Hampshire.

Most of Connecticut's early settlers were also Massachusetts people. Many were seeking greater religious freedom, although quite a few were just looking for a place where they would have more opportunities. Massachusetts officials wanted Connecticut to be settled to prevent the Dutch from taking control of the region. In early fall of 1633, men from Massachusetts were sent to build a fortified trading post in Connecticut a few miles north of the House of Hope. Feeling that the trading post offered some protection, many Massachusetts people soon began moving to Connecticut.

# CONNECTICUT'S THREE RIVER TOWNS AND OLD SAYBROOK

Connecticut's first permanent English town was Windsor, which was founded in 1633 around the English trading post near the House of Hope. Windsor's early settlers included many people who had left Massachusetts because of religious restrictions.

Wethersfield was settled in 1634, just a year after Windsor. It was founded by a few Massachusetts people who hoped they could make a better life by trading with the Indians and farming there.

Hartford (Connecticut's capital today) was first permanently settled in 1635. Among its early colonists were people led by the Reverend Thomas Hooker of Newtowne (now Cambridge), Massachusetts. More open-minded about religion than Massachusetts officials, Hooker wanted to build a place where his congregation could live in peace.

Thomas Hooker

Hooker and over 100 of his followers left Newtowne, Massachusetts, in late spring of 1636. They sang psalms as they traveled through the forest toward Connecticut. During the two weeks that it took the group to reach Hartford, they lived mainly on milk from the cows they had brought along, and on food provided by the Indians.

Although about sixty people had settled there a few months earlier in late 1635, Thomas Hooker is considered Hartford's founder because he did so much to make it into a town.

A fourth settlement, Old Saybrook, was founded in late 1635 by a group of rich Englishmen called the Company of Lords and Gentlemen. It was intended as a haven for wealthy Puritans from England. However, George Fenwick was the only Puritan aristocrat to move there from England, and in its first years Old Saybrook was mainly a military fort and trading post.

English settlers took land from the Dutch. They tore down a Dutch shield and carved a grinning face in its place. They named their settlement Old Saybrook.

Early Connecticut colonists traveled from Massachusetts Bay in the cold and snow.

Connecticut's first colonists endured many hardships. The few who had arrived by late 1635 suffered through a very cold winter. Ships could not get through the frozen Connecticut River, and food ran low. Fortunately, friendly Indians supplied the colonists with food, which helped them survive until spring.

Some of the poorer colonists could not build houses at first. Instead, they built what were called "dugouts" or "cellars." To construct a dugout, the family dug a pit in a hillside. They lined the sides of the pit with logs or stones for walls. The roof was made of tree bark and poles held together with clay plaster.

The colonists cut down trees to build houses and barns.

Spinning wheels were used to spin wool and flax into yarn.

As soon as they could, the dugout dwellers and the other Connecticut colonists built wooden houses. Connecticut had no shortage of wood, the main building material of colonial times. In fact, early Connecticut was said to have so many trees that a squirrel could cross almost the whole colony without touching the ground.

The colonists chopped down trees and used the wood to build their houses. Each house had at least one fireplace made of clay bricks or stone. The fireplace heated the house during Connecticut's cold winters. Food was cooked in large pots suspended over the fireplace.

Each family also cut down timber to make way for crops. Connecticut's early colonists grew corn, wheat, rye, and assorted vegetables. Cows they had brought with them to Connecticut provided milk. Nearly every family also hunted and fished for some of their food, much like their Indian neighbors.

Windsor, Wethersfield, and Hartford were called the Three River Towns because they were all located on the Connecticut River within about fifteen miles of one another. In the spring of 1636, these three towns joined together to form the Connecticut Colony. They created a government, called the Connecticut General Court, which first met in April of 1636. The settlement at Old Saybrook was a separate colony.

Work was done by hand.

## THE PEQUOT WAR

The Indian tribes along the Connecticut River, known as the River Tribes, included the Tunxis, the Podunk, and the Wangunk. The River Tribes were for the most part friendly and helpful toward the newcomers.

The Pequots, who lived in what is now southeastern Connecticut, had about as many people as all of Connecticut's other tribes combined. Known for their fierceness in war, the Pequots were very upset to see settlers streaming into Connecticut. They realized that the flood of colonists might eventually push them off their lands.

Several events triggered a war between the Pequots and the colonists. In 1634, the Pequots—or Indians taking orders from them—killed Captain John Stone, a trader. It was reported that Stone had mistreated the Indians. Possibly the Pequots thought Stone was a Dutchman. The Pequots had a grudge against the Dutch (who remained at the House of Hope until 1653) for murdering an Indian sachem.

Two years later, in 1636, some Indians killed Captain John Oldham, a trader who was one of the founders of Wethersfield. Although the Pequots had not murdered Oldham, they would not turn over the men who had. In revenge, the English murdered several Pequots and destroyed Pequot homes and crops. The Pequots then took up arms against the English. Fought in 1636–1637, this Pequot War was one of the most tragic events in the history of the Thirteen Colonies.

The Pequots attacked Wethersfield and Old Saybrook as well as other Connecticut settlements in late 1636 and early 1637. By spring of 1637 about two dozen colonists had died at the Pequots' hands. In May of 1637, the Connecticut

Captain Mason's expedition attacks the Pequot village.

colonists held an emergency General Court meeting at Hartford. Captain John Mason of Windsor was placed in charge of nearly 100 men. Several hundred Indian friends joined this army. Most of them were Narragansets from Rhode Island, and about 60 were Mohegans. The Mohegans had been part of the Pequots, but at the start of the Pequot War they had broken away as a separate tribe under Chief Uncas.

In early June of 1637, Captain Mason and his soldiers, along with their Indian friends, approached a large Indian village near what is now West Mystic, Connecticut. At dawn on June 5, 1637, the colonial forces set the Pequot village ablaze. About 700 Pequots were burned to death, while only a handful escaped. This was one of the worst slaughters of defenseless people ever perpetrated in what is now the United States.

During the next few weeks, the colonial forces killed and captured hundreds of other Pequots. Not only were the Pequots utterly beaten in this war, they were nearly destroyed as a people. Most of the Pequot survivors were sold as slaves to tribes that were friendly to the English. Connecticut's other Indians were so shocked by the Englishmen's cruelty that any thoughts of opposing them were driven from their minds.

## THE FOUNDING OF NEW HAVEN

John Davenport

After the Pequot War ended, more and more colonists were attracted to Connecticut. About the time that the fighting ended in July of 1637, a group of wealthy Puritans arrived in Boston, Massachusetts, from England. The Puritans were led by the Reverend John Davenport and Theophilus Eaton.

At the time, there was a controversy over Anne Hutchinson's religious teachings in Boston. Some people favored Mrs. Hutchinson, who believed in a more loving God and greater religious freedom than did most Massachusetts leaders. A growing number of people opposed her.

The Puritans locked people in the pillory as a punishment for minor offenses.

Our society today thrives on disagreements. We argue about many matters from politics to sports. But in the 1630s most colonists thought that only one way of thinking should be allowed concerning religion and other important matters. The Reverend Davenport and his group opposed Anne Hutchinson, and were troubled by all the arguing over her views. They decided to move to a place where Puritan ideas wouldn't be challenged.

Returning soldiers from the Pequot War told other Massachusetts people about a beautiful region of Connecticut on Long Island Sound. In late summer of 1637, Theophilus Eaton led an exploring group from Massachusetts to southern Connecticut. They came to a region where the Quinnipiac Indians lived and where a river named the Quinnipiac flowed into Long Island Sound. They chose this place for their new home.

Other Massachusetts people decided to make the move with the Davenport-Eaton group. In spring of 1638, dozens of people sailed from Boston in several small boats. Because of bad weather, it took two weeks to make the rather short trip. Soon after landing at the place where the Quinnipiac River empties into Long Island Sound, they began building a colony. At first the colony was called Quinnipiac, but in 1640 its

The settlers held a religious service on their first Sunday at New Haven.

A home in New Haven in 1637

name was changed to New Haven, after Newhaven, England.

By 1638 there were three separate English colonies in what is now Connecticut. There was the Connecticut Colony, composed of the river towns, and the colonies of Old Saybrook and New Haven.

Thomas Hooker and his
followers traveled for two weeks
through the wilderness to
Hartford, crossing mountains
and swamps and fording rivers.
Mrs. Hooker rode on a litter.

# Chapter IV

## The Young, Growing Colony: 1638-1675

*The foundation of authority is laid, firstly, in the free consent of the people.*

*Thomas Hooker, speaking in 1638*

Thomas Hooker, the main founder of Hartford, was in many ways a man ahead of his time. Most Puritans felt that lawmakers were God's agents on earth and that they had the right to dictate most aspects of people's lives. Hooker, on the other hand, felt that people could limit their lawmakers' power and that the lawmakers should account to the people for their actions. In other words, he felt that citizens should play a larger role in government than most Puritans thought was proper.

In spring of 1638, the Reverend Hooker preached a sermon on these topics at Hartford. During this sermon, Hooker spoke the words heading this chapter about authority coming from "the free consent of the people." These words seem to lift Hooker out of the 1630s and into the 1770s, when the United States was being created.

For in the Declaration of Independence, which Thomas Jefferson wrote in 1776, similar words were used to explain that the people are the source of authority:

> *... to secure these rights, Governments are instituted among Men, deriving their just powers from the consent of the [people who are] governed. ...*

Thomas Hooker's sermon became widely known. Soon after he gave it, the Connecticut General Court made a set of laws for the colony based on Hooker's ideas. Known as the Fundamental Orders, these laws were probably written by Roger Ludlow, who was said to be the colony's only trained lawyer at the time. Representatives of the Connecticut Colony's towns approved the Fundamental Orders at a meeting in Hartford on January 14, 1639.

The first church in Connecticut, built at Hartford in 1638

Some historians have called the Fundamental Orders the first constitution (set of important laws) enacted in what is now the United States. Ideas expressed in the Fundamental Orders later became part of other colonial and state constitutions. And Thomas Jefferson used ideas from those documents in the Declaration of Independence. So, by a chain reaction, Thomas Hooker really did leap out of the 1630s and

Representatives from Hartford, Wethersfield, and Windsor met to draw up a constitution, the Fundamental Orders of Connecticut.

influence the ideas in the Declaration of Independence in 1776.

The Fundamental Orders offered nowhere near the freedom Americans enjoy today. As was typical in the Thirteen Colonies, only men who owned property could vote or hold office, with the result that all women and most men were excluded from politics. But, for their time, the Fundamental Orders offered people a great deal of freedom. For example, the Orders placed no religious restrictions on voting, unlike the laws in other colonies. The Orders also barred the governor from serving two terms in a row, so that he wouldn't become too powerful. Connecticut people liked the Fundamental Orders so much that they kept them in effect until 1662, when a very famous set of laws took their place.

Meanwhile, the New Haven Colony to the southwest was being run much differently. New Haven people could not vote, and they had far less say in their government than did the Connecticut Colony people. New Haven was a theocracy—its religious leaders were also its political leaders. Biblical law was so important in New Haven that the colony was nicknamed the Bible State.

Thus Connecticut appealed to a variety of people. For those seeking a strict Puritan life, it had the New Haven Colony. For those seeking more freedom than was offered in Massachusetts or New Haven, there was the Connecticut Colony. The region that is now Connecticut also had plenty of land for people who wanted to farm, timber for those who wanted to build ships, and waterways for those who hoped to fish or ship merchandise for a living.

These attractions lured several thousand people to Connecticut, mainly from England and Massachusetts, between 1640 and 1660. During those years the population of what is now Connecticut

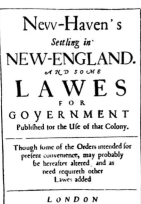

Laws for the colony of New Haven were drawn up by Governor Eaton in 1656.

grew from about 1,500 to about 8,000. Eight thousand people may sound like a small population to us, because the United States now has cities that have hundreds of times as many people. But in 1660, only about 75,000 people lived in all of England's American colonies.

Connecticut people did not all stay in the original towns. They soon fanned out across the countryside and built new towns. The following are towns that by 1660 were part of the Connecticut Colony and the less powerful New Haven Colony:

| Connecticut Colony | New Haven Colony |
| --- | --- |
| Windsor (founded in 1633) | New Haven (settled in 1638) |
| Wethersfield (settled in 1634) | Guilford (founded in 1639) |
| Hartford (settled in 1635) | Milford (founded in 1639) |
| Old Saybrook (founded in 1635) | Greenwich (settled in 1640) |
| Fairfield (settled in 1639) | Southold (founded in 1640) |
| Farmington (settled in 1640) | Stamford (settled in 1641) |
| New London (settled in 1646) | Branford (settled in 1644) |
| Norwalk (settled in 1649) | |
| Middletown (settled in 1650) | |

Old Saybrook had been founded as a separate colony in 1635. But Old Saybrook had done poorly as an independent colony, and in late 1644 George Fenwick sold it to the Connecticut Colony.

If you look at a map of Connecticut, you can find all the cities and towns mentioned above except for Southold. Southold can be found on Long Island in what is now New York state. For part of the 1600s, Connecticut claimed the towns on the eastern end of Long Island, so Southold and some other towns that are now in New York state were considered part of Connecticut in its early years.

During the 1600s and the 1700s, England's American colonies argued a great deal with one another over their borders. Some of the strange zigzags that can be seen on maps of the eastern states resulted from compromises that colonies made over their borders. For example, Greenwich, in what is now far southwestern Connecticut, was settled in 1640 by New Haven people. But New York also wanted the Greenwich area, and for years the town bounced around between Connecticut and New York like a Ping-Pong ball. Finally, the two colonies agreed in 1683 that Greenwich would be part of Connecticut. The border the two colonies worked out gave Connecticut the odd-shaped "handle" located in its southwestern corner.

Stonington was another town that became involved in a tug-of-war between two colonies. Located in what is now far southeastern Connecticut near the Rhode Island border, Stonington was founded in 1649. Massachusetts, which claimed

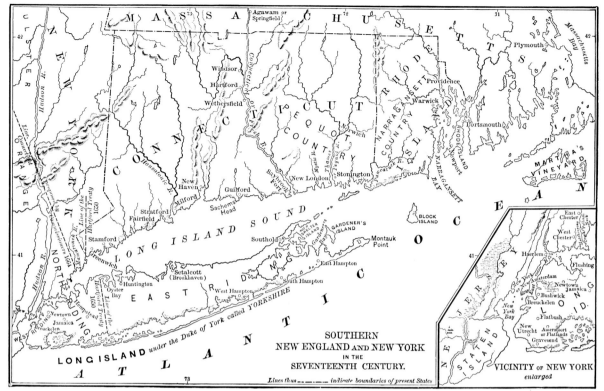

SOUTHERN
NEW ENGLAND AND NEW YORK
IN THE
SEVENTEENTH CENTURY.

Lines thus _ _ _ . _ _ indicate boundaries of present States

VICINITY OF NEW YORK
enlarged

This map shows Massachusets, Connecticut, and Rhode Island in the 17th century.

parts of Rhode Island, claimed the Stonington region. Connecticut and Massachusetts argued over Stonington for years until the town officially became part of Connecticut in 1662.

Land for Connecticut's towns had to be obtained from the Indians. The Pequots were no longer a factor, having been nearly destroyed during the Pequot War of 1636–1637. The other tribes were taken advantage of in land deals throughout the Thirteen Colonies and then pushed out of their ancestral homes.

The Indians felt that the ground, like the air, could be used but not owned, so the very idea of

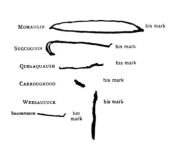

Indians signed documents by "making a mark." Each person had a special mark.

selling land was foreign to them. When making land deals, the Indians usually thought they were agreeing to *share* rather than *sell* the land. The contracts were in English, and so the Indians were at a disadvantage when it came to understanding the wording. The Indians were often shocked to learn that they were no longer allowed on the land of their birth. When the Indians complained, the English showed them the papers they had signed giving up their land forever.

If the Indians did not want to sign away their lands, the colonists might give them liquor to soften them up. In Connecticut, fines were also used to get the Indians' land. As the Indians lost their hunting grounds, they had trouble feeding their families. Sometimes, Indians stole vegetables from the colonists' fields, or broke other colonial laws. What was the fine the Indians were ordered to pay when they were caught? More land!

A number of Connecticut towns were built on land purchased from the Indians for tiny payments. In late 1638 the New Haven colonists bought a large piece of land from the Quinnipiac Indians that included present-day New Haven, North Haven, Wallingford, Cheshire, Hamden, Bethany, and Orange. The colonists paid 24 coats, 12 spoons, 12 hatchets, 12 hoes, 24 knives, 12 bowls, and 4 cases of French knives and scissors for this land. This deal was made in the cold months of November and December, when the 24 coats meant a great deal to the Indians.

In 1640, the land that Greenwich was built on was purchased from the Indians for 25 coats. That same year, a large area that included Norwalk was bought from the Indians for 6 coats, 10 hatchets, 10 hoes, 10 knives, 10 scissors, 10 musical instruments called Jew's harps, 10 mirrors, 3 kettles, some tobacco, and some wampum beads. It was also said that during the late 1600s a tract of land on which the town of Danbury was built was bought from the Indians for one bag of beans. Although this was probably a tall tale, it shows how the colonists expected to obtain land very cheaply from the Indians.

Eunice Mauwee, the last surviving Pequot Indian, was 100 years old when this painting was made in 1852.

It should be added that not all of the English people who dealt with the Indians set out to take advantage of them. There was a widespread feeling that there would always be plenty of land left for the Indians. But as more towns were built, most of the Indians were gradually squeezed out of Connecticut.

The Connecticut colonists made many improvements in their way of life as their numbers grew. For one thing, they built larger and stronger

The Reverend Whitfield
House in Guilford

houses. A famous Connecticut landmark, the
Reverend Whitfield House, was built in 1639–
1640 in the town of Guilford. It is the oldest stone
house still standing in New England.

Connecticut people also quickly developed a
fine educational system. The Puritans were
among the most education-minded people in
history. They felt that young people must be
educated in order to read and understand the
Bible. In 1636, the Massachusetts Puritans
founded Harvard, the first college in what is now
the United States. And in 1647, Massachusetts
made a law requiring each town with at least fifty
families to have a school that was paid for in part

by tax money. This was the start of the American public school system.

Various towns in the Connecticut and the New Haven colonies voluntarily set up schools during the late 1630s and the 1640s. But both colonies wanted to have laws that would require towns to set up schools. In 1650, the Connecticut Colony passed a law much like Massachusetts' public school law of 1647. All Connecticut towns with at least fifty families had to set up public schools where boys and girls would learn reading and writing. All towns with at least 100 families had to set up secondary schools similar to our high schools, where Latin and other advanced subjects would be taught. In 1656-1657, the New Haven Colony also passed laws requiring its towns to maintain public schools.

The purpose of the secondary schools was to prepare young men for college. (In colonial times, young women were not allowed to go to college.) Until 1701, Connecticut had no college of its own, but some of its young men went to Harvard College near Boston, Massachusetts. And some of Connecticut's richer families sent a portion of their corn crop (called "college corn") to Harvard each year to help support the college.

A colonial school

Hornbooks were used in colonial schools. Since paper was scarce and expensive, the lessons were pasted to a wooden board and protected by a thin sheet of horn.

Connecticut's focus on education yielded good results. In some of the Thirteen Colonies, there were few schools and only a small portion of the population could read and write. Comparatively speaking, Connecticut had many schools, and a high percentage of its young people learned to read and write.

## THE KING GRANTS CONNECTICUT A CHARTER

In England, during the 1650s, the Puritans had been in charge of the government. Then in 1660, the Puritans lost power in England. This worried the Puritans across the Atlantic Ocean who comprised the bulk of Connecticut's population. What if the new king, Charles II, decided to let the powerful Massachusetts Colony take control of Connecticut? What if the Dutch who controlled New York tried to take over Connecticut and the king did not stop them?

Connecticut people decided that they needed a charter, like Massachusetts had, to protect them. This paper would state that Connecticut people had a right to be there, and it would specify the colony's type of government and boundaries. The Connecticut General Court voted to ask the king for a charter in early spring of 1661.

Charles II ruled from 1660 to 1685.

John Winthrop, Jr., was the governor of Connecticut at the time. He was so popular that in
1660 the General Court had voted to end the rule
preventing a governor from serving two terms in a
row so that Winthrop could keep serving as
governor. Winthrop was also very charming and
intelligent. It was decided that he would sail to
England and ask the king for a charter. It must be
kept in mind that he was supporting the interests
of the Connecticut Colony rather than the less
powerful New Haven Colony.

John Winthrop, Jr.

Winthrop sailed to England in the summer of
1661. He soon showed that Connecticut had
picked the right man for the job. King Charles II
liked Governor Winthrop very much. At the end of
their meeting, the Connecticut governor left some
papers with the king. These papers explained the
rights, privileges, and borders that Connecticut
hoped to have.

On April 23, 1662, Charles II signed a charter
granting Connecticut all that it had wanted. The
Connecticut colonists were to govern themselves
with little interference from England. Not only
was Connecticut to swallow up the New Haven
Colony, but it was also granted an additional
gigantic tract of land. Connecticut's northern and

southern borders would be the same basic boundaries that the state has today. But Connecticut's eastern border was to be Narragansett Bay, giving it most of Rhode Island! Connecticut's western border was the real shocker, though. Connecticut was to extend west all the way to the Pacific Ocean!

How could the king grant Connecticut so much land? For one thing, he probably knew less about American geography than the average fourth-grader today. For another, he seems to have liked Governor Winthrop enough to have granted him just about anything.

If the charter of Charles II had been adopted, Connecticut would stretch from the Atlantic to the Pacific Ocean.

Imagine what the U. S. map would look like today if all that land had really become part of Connecticut. The state would be about 70 miles from north to south and 3,000 miles from east to west. Its total area of 210,000 square miles would make Connecticut the third-largest (instead of the third-smallest) state, behind only Alaska and Texas. Connecticut would also be the weirdest-shaped state by far! Besides Rhode Island, parts of the states of New York, Pennsylvania, Ohio, Indiana, Illinois, Iowa, Nebraska, Wyoming, Utah, Nevada, and California would all be part of Connecticut. Instead of being in Ohio and Illinois, the cities of Cleveland and Chicago would both be in

Connecticut. California's Mount Shasta and a good portion of Utah's Great Salt Lake would also be in Connecticut.

Of course, Connecticut does not own most of Rhode Island, and its western border ends almost 3,000 miles east of the Pacific Ocean. Over the years, Connecticut tried to claim only small portions of land beyond its present borders, but the state eventually gave up those claims.

John Winthrop, Jr., stayed a few more months in England to take care of some business. Meanwhile, he shipped the charter to America. Before reaching Connecticut, the charter went to Boston, where the New England Confederation was meeting. Comprised of the Massachusetts, Plymouth (until 1691 the Plymouth Colony was separate from the Massachusetts Colony), Connecticut, and New Haven colonies, this organization worked to solve border disputes and to protect New England from outside attack. The charter was soon brought to Hartford, where it was first read aloud publicly in October of 1662.

Connecticut's huge land grant led to border disputes with Rhode Island and New York that took many years to resolve. As for Connecticut's far western lands, the Connecticut colonists might as well have been told they owned the moon for all it meant to them. Many years would pass before settlers moved into most of those western lands. The big news to the Connecticut people of 1662 was that New Haven was supposed to be merged with the Connecticut Colony.

The people in the New Haven Colony had tried to obtain a separate charter for their colony back in 1647. However, the ship carrying New Haven's representative had sunk before reaching England. After that, the colony had done little about obtaining its own charter.

James, Duke of York

When they learned that their colony was to be swallowed by Connecticut, many New Haven people were angry. Connecticut Colony officials tried to reassure them. They promised that Connecticut would leave New Haven churches alone. And they promised that New Haven could send a fair share of representatives to the General Assembly, the new name for the General Court. However, a number of New Haven people wanted to move rather than become part of Connecticut, and some were ready to fight.

Events in England and in nearby colonies changed the attitude of many New Haven Colony people. In 1664, England's King Charles II gave a large tract of American land to his brother James, the Duke of York. Most of this land comprised what are now the states of New York, New Jersey, and Delaware, all of which the Dutch ruled as New Netherland. In 1664, James sent a fleet of warships to take control of New Netherland. New York, New Jersey, and Delaware thus passed from Dutch to English control.

There was one shocking aspect to the gift of land that Charles II had made to his brother. It included most of what is now Connecticut. Charles II had granted Connecticut to two different owners. In 1662, he granted it to the Connecticut Colony people. Then in 1664, he gave it to his brother, the Duke of York.

There is an old saying about choosing the "lesser of two evils." And there is another old saying about there being "strength in numbers." New Haven Colony people saw that the Duke of York might want their lands. They knew that they and the Connecticut Colony would have a better chance of fighting off this challenge if they banded together. And most New Haven people felt that becoming part of the Connecticut Colony was not as bad as becoming part of New York. These were the main reasons why the New Haven Colony joined the Connecticut Colony in late 1664. Also that year, the Duke of York made a deal with Connecticut. He released his claim to Connecticut, and in exchange Connecticut gave up its claim to Long Island.

## A VERY SUCCESSFUL COLONY

Connecticut enjoyed growth and great success during the 1660s and early 1670s. Under its charter, Connecticut in many ways was more like an independent country than a colony under England's control. One interesting law was that each Connecticut town could send two representatives to the General Assembly. This meant that the small towns had as much power as the larger ones.

Connecticut farmers were having great success growing corn, wheat, peas, and tobacco. Its

Farmers plowing with oxen. The many tree stumps show that this field was cleared from the forest.

fishermen were bringing home tons of fish from Long Island Sound. And ships from Connecticut were also going out into the Atlantic Ocean after whales. These animals were in great demand because whale oil was used in lamps and whalebones were used in making umbrellas and clothing.

Connecticut people were doing so well that many were able to sell a portion of their extra products to England. In return they obtained clothing, tools, and other items from the mother country.

Its success attracted more and more people to Connecticut. By 1670, about 13,000 colonists lived in Connecticut. That was also about the population of Maryland. The only colonies with more people were the two oldest ones, Virginia and Massachusetts.

# JOHN WINTHROP, JR. (1606–1676)

John Winthrop, Jr.

John Winthrop, the founder of Boston, Massachusetts, had a total of at least sixteen children by four different wives. In those days it was common for a man or woman who reached old age to outlive several wives or husbands, and for families to be very large.

The first of John Winthrop's sixteen children was John Winthrop, Jr., who was born in Groton, England, in 1606. When John, Jr., was nine years old, his mother died. He was raised mainly by his father and by a stepmother whom he came to deeply love.

John, Jr., went to several schools in England and then to Trinity College in Dublin, Ireland. Later, he studied law in England, but found that he had little interest in being a lawyer. He gave up law and in the spring of 1627 joined the English navy as secretary to a ship captain. He sailed to France on a war expedition that proved to be a total failure for England. Feeling restless, and still undecided about his career, John, Jr., then went on a one-year European tour in which he visited France, Germany, The Netherlands, Italy, and Turkey.

When he returned to England in 1629, John Winthrop, Jr., found that his father was planning to lead about 1,000 Puritans from England to Massachusetts. John Winthrop made this journey in the spring of 1630. While his father was founding Boston, John, Jr., stayed in England for a while to care for younger family members and to oversee family business. Then in the summer of 1631, John Winthrop, Jr., sailed to New England with his wife, Martha, and many other family members.

After a ten-week voyage, their ship reached Boston. While in Massachusetts, John Winthrop, Jr., founded the town of Ipswich. During a trip back to England in 1635, he was appointed to build a new settlement in Connecticut. He founded this settlement, Old Saybrook, in late 1635. During the next few years, though, he lived mainly in what are now Massachusetts and New York. In 1646 he founded the town of New London, Connecticut, and three years later he moved permanently to Connecticut.

Loved and respected by most Connecticut people, John Winthrop, Jr., served as the colony's governor for nearly twenty years. His father was often harsh to people who didn't agree with his religious views. But John Winthrop, Jr., was kind toward such people. His friendly manner helped him obtain the famous Connecticut charter from King Charles II in 1662.

Besides serving so long as Connecticut governor, John Winthrop, Jr., was keenly interested in science. He observed the heavens with several of the first telescopes in North America. And since there was a doctor shortage in the colonies, he studied medicine and treated hundreds of patients, often with great success.

At least three times, John Winthrop, Jr., asked to step down from the Connecticut governorship so that he could take care of business affairs. Each time, the people of Connecticut convinced him to stay because they needed him. He was still governor of Connecticut when he died in 1676 at the age of 70.

John Winthrop, Jr., had outlived two wives—Martha and then Elizabeth. He and Elizabeth had seven children. Their son Fitz-John Winthrop was governor of Connecticut from 1698 to 1707. Their other son, Wait-Still Winthrop, served as chief justice of the Massachusetts Colony.

Saybrook, Connecticut

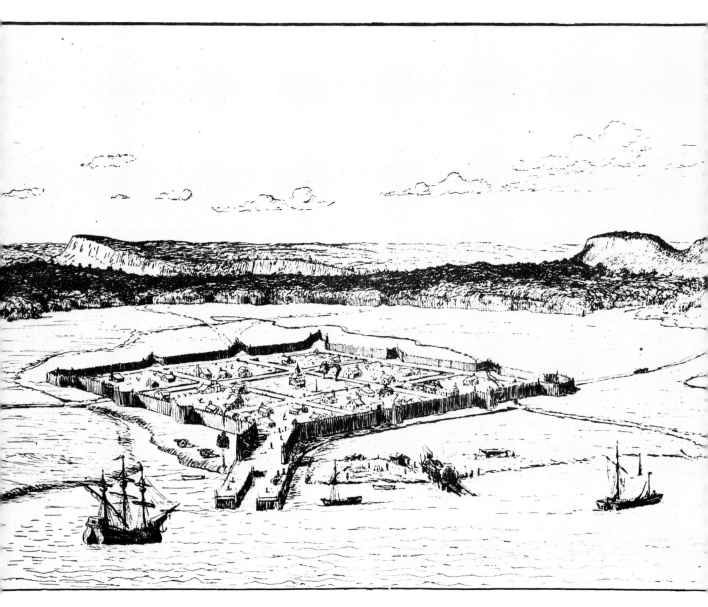

A wall of upright logs called a palisade protected New Haven from
Indian attacks in 1675.

# Chapter V

# Threats to the Colony: 1675-1689

*The charter was brought and laid upon the table, where the assembly were sitting. [Just as Edmund Andros, the enemy of Connecticut, was about to grab the charter] the lights were instantly extinguished, and one Captain Wadsworth, of Hartford, in the most silent and secret manner, carried off the charter, and secreted it in a large hollow tree. . . .*

*The famous story of how Connecticut people refused to give up their charter, as told by Benjamin Trumbull in* A Complete History of Connecticut *(1818)*

## KING PHILIP'S WAR

Connecticut's peace and prosperity were threatened in two big ways in 1675. One threat came from Indians in the neighboring Rhode Island and Massachusetts colonies. The other threat came from an English official who hoped to seize control of Connecticut.

An Indian chief named Metacomet had become very angry at the New England colonists during the 1660s and early 1670s. Metacomet, who was chief of the Wampanoag Indians of Massachusetts and Rhode Island, had reason to feel that way.

Massasoit helped the Pilgrims.

King Philip (Metacomet)

Metacomet's father, Chief Massasoit, had welcomed the Pilgrims soon after their arrival in Plymouth, Massachusetts, in 1620. In fact, without the friendship of Massasoit and another Indian named Squanto, the Pilgrims might not have survived.

Over the years, the New England colonists had repaid the Indians' kindness with cruelty. They had taken more and more of the Indians' lands. They had forced many Indians to become Christians. And many of them had mistreated the Indians in other ways. Something else filled Metacomet with even more hatred. He suspected that the colonists in Massachusetts had murdered his brother.

In 1675-1676, Chief Metacomet led his Wampanoags plus the Narraganset Indians of Rhode Island and several other tribes against the colonists. Metacomet's goal was to drive the colonists out of New England. The colonists' name for Metacomet was King Philip, and so they called the war that he and his people waged against them in 1675-1676 King Philip's War.

Most of the fighting in King Philip's War took place in what is now Massachusetts and Rhode Island. The only raid the Indians made into Connecticut resulted in the burning of the town of

The colonists attack an Indian fortress.

Simsbury, with no deaths occurring. However, as a member of the New England Confederation, Connecticut was expected to supply soldiers to fight King Philip, as he is usually known in history books. Several hundred Connecticut soldiers and over 100 of their Mohegan allies joined the colonial army that fought Philip and his people.

In December of 1675, a 1,000-man New England army, made up mainly of Massachusetts and Connecticut troops, marched to an Indian village near what is now Kingston, Rhode Island. About 3,000 Narraganset Indians and their friends were spending the winter in this village. The colonial army set the village ablaze, burning to death hundreds of Indians, both adults and children.

Hundreds more were shot to death as they ran away. The death toll was even higher than it had been at the slaughter of the Pequots in Connecticut thirty-eight years earlier. About a thousand Indians were massacred in this Great Swamp Fight, as it is called.

The Indians managed to fight back somewhat while they were being massacred. They killed or wounded several hundred colonial soldiers, many of them Connecticut men.

In 1676, Connecticut again sent several hundred soldiers to finish off the war against the Indians. That spring, the Narraganset Chief Canonchet was captured by Connecticut forces, who reportedly offered to spare his life if he made his people surrender. Canonchet refused, saying, "Killing me will not end the war. Others were as forward for the war as myself, and I desire to hear no more about it. Have not the English burned my people in their houses?" Canonchet was then executed in southeastern Connecticut.

Several months later, Philip's wife and son were captured in Massachusetts. They were sold into slavery with other captured Indians. "My heart is broken. I am ready to die," Philip reportedly said after this. A few days later, on August 12, 1676, colonial forces tracked Philip down in Rhode

Island and killed him. Soon after, King Philip's War ended in most of New England.

## THE CHARTER OAK

The Duke of York had agreed to release his claim to Connecticut back in 1664. But ten years later he changed his mind. In 1674, the Duke of York appointed the Englishman Edmund Andros governor of New York. In mid-1675, the Duke of York sent Governor Andros to Connecticut. Andros was to claim all of Connecticut west of the Connecticut River for the duke.

Sir Edmund Andros

In July of 1675, officials at Hartford learned that Andros and some soldiers had left New York and were crossing Long Island Sound in armed boats. Their destination was Old Saybrook, at the mouth of the Connecticut River. If Andros could seize the Old Saybrook fort, he would have a base from which he could later seize Hartford and other Connecticut towns farther up the river.

Officials at Hartford sent militiamen to the Old Saybrook fort. The leader of these soldiers was Captain Thomas Bull of Hartford. Captain Bull ordered his men to ". . . avoid striking the first blow; but if they begin, then you are to defend yourselves. . . ."

New York's Governor Andros arrived at Old

Saybrook around July 9, 1675. On July 11, Andros aimed his boats' guns at the fort and ordered that it be surrendered. King Philip's War had begun just a few days earlier. Instead of admitting that he wanted to take over most of Connecticut for the Duke of York, Andros made it sound as if he had come to direct the defense of Connecticut against the Indians.

Not taken in by this trick, Captain Bull refused to surrender the fort. For a while both Captain Bull and Governor Andros stood their ground, but then they agreed to meet ashore. During their talk, Andros had an aide read a paper stating that the Duke of York claimed western Connecticut.

Captain Bull (left) meets with Governor Andros.

## BY HIS EXCELLENCY
### A
# PROCLAMATION.

WHEREAS His MAJESTY hath been gracioufly pleafed, by His Royal Letter, bearing Date the fixteenth day of October laft paft, to fignifie That He hath received undoubted Advice that a great and fudden Invafion from *Holland*, with an armed Force of Forreigners and Strangers, will fpeedily be made in an hoftile manner upon His Majefty's Kingdom of *ENGLAND*; and that altho' fome *falfe* pretences relating to *Liberty, Property,* and *Religion,* (contrived or worded with Art and Subtilty) may be given out, (as fhall be thought ufeful upon fuch an Attempt; ) It is manifeft however, (confidering the great Preparations that are making) That no lefs matter by this *Invafion* is propofed and purpofed, than an abfolute Conqueft of His Majefty's Kingdoms, and the utter Subduing and Subjecting His Majefty and all His People to a Forreign Power, which is promoted (as His Majefty underftands) altho' it may feem almoft incredible) by fome of His Majefty's *Subjects,* being perfons of wicked and reftlefs Spirits, implacable Malice, and defperate Defigns, who having no fence of former inteftine Diftractions, (the Memory and Mifery whereof fhould endear and put a Value upon that Peace and Happinefs which hath long been enjoyed) nor being moved by His Majefty's reiterated Acts of Grace and Mercy, (wherein His Majefty hath ftudied and delighted to abound towards all His Subjects, and even towards *thofe* who were once His Majefty's avowed and open *Enemies*) do again endeavour to embroil His Majefty's Kingdom in Blood and Ruin, to gratifie their own Ambition and Malice, propofing to themfelves a Prey and Booty in fuch a publick Confufion:

And that although His Majefty had Notice that a forreign Force was preparing againft Him, yet His Majefty hath alwaies declined any forreign Succour, but rather hath chofen (next under- GOD) to rely upon the true and ancient Courage, Faith and Allegiance of His own People, with whom His Majefty hath often ventured His Life for the Honour of His Nation, and in whofe Defence againft all Enemies His Majefty is firmly refolved to live and dye; and therefore does folemnly *Conjure* His Subjects to lay afide all manner of Animofities, Jealoufies, & Prejudices, and heartily & chearfully to *Unite together* in the Defence of His *MAJESTY* and their native Countrey, which thing alone, will (under GOD) defeat and fruftrate the principal Hope and Defign of His Majefty's Enemies, who expect to find His People divided; and by publifhing (perhaps) fome plaufible Reafons of their Coming, as the fpecious (tho' *falfe*) Pretences of Maintaining the Proteftant Religion, or Afferting the Liberties and Properties of His Majefty's People, do hope thereby to conquer that great and renowned Kingdom.

That albeit the Defign hath been carried on with all imaginable Secrefie & Endeavours to furprife and deceive His *MAJESTY,* HE hath not been wanting on His part to make fuch provifion as did become Him, and, by GOD's great Bleffing, His Majefty makes no doubt of being found in fo good a Pofture that His Enemies may have caufe to repent fuch their rafh and *injuft* Attempt. ALL WHICH, it is His Majefty's pleafure, fhould be made known in the moft publick manner to His loving Subjects within this His Territory and Dominion of *NEW-ENGLAND,* that they may be the better prepared to refift any Attempts that may be made by His Majefties Enemies in thefe parts, and fecured in their trade and Commerce with His Majefty's Kingdom of *England.*

I Do therefore, in purfuance of His *MAJESTY's* Commands, by thefe Prefents *make known* and *Publifh* the fame accordingly: And hereby Charge and Command all Officers Civil & Military, and all other His Majefty's loving Subjects within this His Territory and Dominion aforefaid, to be *Vigilant* and *Careful* in their refpective places and ftations, and that, upon the Approach of any Fleet or Forreign Force, they be in Readinefs, and ufe their utmoft Endeavour to hinder any Landing or Invafion that may be intended to be made within the fame.

Given at *Fort-Charles* at *Pemaquid,* the Tenth Day of *January,* in the Fourth year of the Reign of our Sovereign Lord *JAMES* the Second, of *England, Scotland, France* and *Ireland* KING, Defender of the Faith &c. Annoq; DOMINI 1688.

*By. His* EXCELLENCY's *Command.*
*JOHN WEST.* d'. Secr'.

E ANDROS

*GOD SAVE THE KING.*

Printed at *Bofton* in *New-England* by *R. P.*

King James II called on the colonists to defend New England against foreign enemies in this proclamation of 1688.

Captain Bull ordered the aide to stop reading the paper, but the man continued. Bull then repeated his order so forcefully that the man stopped reading. According to tradition, an interesting little conversation then took place between Captain Bull and Governor Andros.

"What is your name?" Governor Andros supposedly asked Bull.

"My name is Bull, sir," answered the captain.

Andros reportedly said, "Bull! It is a pity that your horns are not tipped with silver." This was probably a bribe offer. If Bull and his men would give up the fort, they might be given some silver. But when Bull and his men held firm, Governor Andros and his men headed back across Long Island Sound toward New York. Andros and the Duke of York gave up the idea of seizing Connecticut—for the time being.

Ten years later, in 1685, England's King Charles II died. His brother, James, the Duke of York, then became King James II of England. The trouble Connecticut had experienced from James while he had been the Duke of York was nothing compared with what he stirred up once he was king of England!

In 1686, King James II decided to unite the English colonies in what is now the northeastern United States into a single colony. This would make it easier to defend the region from Indians and other enemies, the king said. And it would make it easier for the people of the region to do business with each other. What the king neglected to say was that it would also help him tighten his grip on the colonies.

In 1686, the king began disbanding the assemblies and other self-governing bodies in Connecticut, Massachusetts, New Hampshire, New Jersey, New York, Plymouth, and Rhode Island. He united these seven colonies into a single province called the Dominion of New England. Boston was the capital of this new supercolony. And as its governor, the king chose none other than his old friend and Connecticut's old foe, Edmund Andros.

Most people in the newly formed colony were angry for at least three reasons. First, they felt that King James II had no right to take away the degree of self-government earlier kings had granted them. Second, just as Americans today have pride in their state, many Americans back then felt pride in their colony and didn't want to be swallowed up by a supercolony. And third, the colonists hated Edmund Andros, who jailed protesters and imposed higher taxes.

It must be mentioned, though, that a minority of people did not oppose the change. In those days, a small number of the wealthier men controlled colonial governments. Some of these

Governor Andros strolls among the people of Boston.

men thought they would maintain their power or perhaps even gain more if they cooperated with the new Andros government. There were also some people who felt that the king's orders must be obeyed no matter what.

Soon after reaching Boston in late 1686, Andros began asking the colonists to turn in their old charters. He was replacing them with new laws that granted the colonists far less freedom. Andros didn't need the old charters to put his new government into effect. He planned to make his changes whether the colonists agreed to them or not. But he hoped the colonists would cooperate.

Several colonies did turn in their charters. Some Connecticut lawmakers favored handing over their charter, too. They either hoped to obtain jobs in Andros's government or felt compelled to obey the king. But many Connecticut people didn't want to part with the charter that John Winthrop had obtained twenty-four years earlier. Although Andros wrote two letters demanding it, these people delayed turning in the charter month after month.

Finally, after nearly a year of these delays, Governor Andros decided to go to Connecticut and take the charter. He and over sixty soldiers arrived in Hartford on the afternoon of October 31, 1687. Andros and his men marched to the legislative meetinghouse, where Connecticut's government was assembled. They were met at the door by Connecticut Governor Robert Treat. Although Treat did not want to give up the charter or see his colony's government dissolved, he apparently was very polite, leading Andros to think that he was cooperating. Governor Treat may have helped plan a trick that was soon played on Governor Andros on that Halloween!

There are many different versions of the story. The one known fact is that Andros was prevented from seizing the charter. According to tradition, the charter was taken right from under Andros's nose and hidden in a big tree that became known as the Charter Oak. The following version of how it happened is based mainly on the writings of Benjamin Trumbull, a Connecticut historian who was born about 200 years ago.

Inside the meetinghouse, Andros told Governor Treat and the Connecticut lawmakers that their government was dissolved. He ordered them to turn in their charter and submit to his new government. Governor Treat began protesting to Andros that this was unfair. He described how Connecticut people had fought Indians, built farms and towns, and achieved much self-government. He even said that turning over the charter would be like giving up his life.

As time passed, candles were brought to provide light for the ongoing discussion. Finally, Andros lost his patience and ordered Treat to bring out the charter. It was spread across the table where Andros was sitting with Treat and other Connecti-

Andros and Treat discuss the Connecticut charter.

cut officials. Just as Andros was about to grab the charter, someone snuffed out the candles. By the time they were relit, the charter was gone. It was thought that during the moments of darkness Captain Joseph Wadsworth had picked up the charter and slipped out through an open window. He reportedly hid it in a hollow oak tree near the home of Samuel Wyllys, a Connecticut official.

The original charter was hidden in the Charter Oak.

The Connecticut charter was kept in this box.

The charter, which remained in the tree until after King James II died in 1701, is now kept in the Connecticut State Library in Hartford. The Charter Oak stood until 1856. In August of that year, the most beloved Connecticut landmark of colonial times was destroyed during the Charter Oak Storm.

Connecticut people have told the Charter Oak story for over 300 years because it shows how strongly they have always guarded their rights. Governor Andros felt differently about this event. After disbanding the Connecticut government, Andros appointed his own officials to rule the region and he also took away some of the people's rights. However, events in England soon toppled Andros from power and broke the Dominion of New England into its original parts.

What happened was that in 1688 King James II was overthrown. Once the news traveled the 3,000 miles across the Atlantic Ocean, New Englanders realized that Andros's source of power was gone. In the spring of 1689, people in Boston, Massachusetts, arrested Andros and other English officials. Andros was shipped back to England. The northern colonies then returned to the old laws that granted them some self-government.

Connecticut's government returned to the way it had been before Andros's arrival on Halloween of 1687, a year and a half earlier. Robert Treat again became governor, and the Assembly and other public offices were filled mainly by the same men who had held these positions before Andros's arrival.

The French surrender the Canadian fortress of Louisbourg.

# Chapter VI

# Colonial Wars, Yale College, and Connecticut Yankees: 1689–1750

*In 1698 it was proposed by several ministers that a college should be founded in Connecticut, as it had long been inconvenient to send young men to Massachusetts for their education. . . . They [ten ministers] met [in 1701] at Branford, where they founded the college, by a contribution of about 40 [books]: Each saying, as he presented his books, "I give these books for the founding of a college in this colony."*

*From* The History of Connecticut, *by Theodore Dwight, Jr. (1841)*

## CONNECTICUT HELPS ENGLAND FIGHT FRANCE

France is England's neighbor to the south across the English Channel. By the late 1600s, France and England had been enemies on and off for centuries. But all their wars had been fought in Europe. In the late 1600s, the two nations began fighting each other in North America.

Rivals in many ways, France and England had begun colonizing North America at about the same time. England had begun the first of its Thirteen Colonies—Virginia—in 1607. France had built Quebec, which is now Canada's oldest city, in 1608. England continued to settle what is now the eastern United States, while France colonized eastern Canada, which it called New France.

By the late 1600s, England and France wanted each other's North American lands. And both countries were eyeing the vast stretch of land in what is now the middle of the United States.

The dotted areas were occupied by the English.

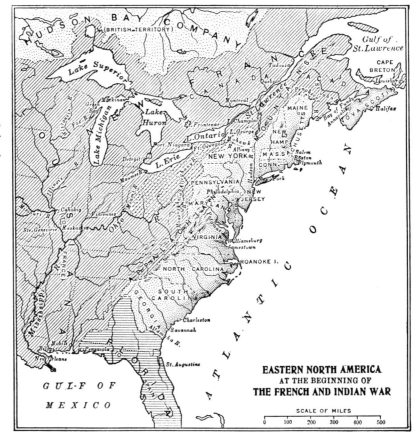

In 1689, England and France began fighting what proved to be four wars for control of North America. The French had generally treated the Indians well, and many Frenchmen had married Indian women. The English had for the most part treated the Indians poorly. As a result, thousands of Indians sided with the French in these wars, although a smaller number of Indians chose the English as their allies. These four wars are often called the Colonial Wars. Specifically, they were:

King William's War (1689-1697)

Queen Anne's War (1702-1713)

King George's War (1744-1748)

The French and Indian War (1754-1763)

Although some English troops crossed the ocean to fight the French and the Indians, most of the fighting was done by men from England's American colonies. And although no fighting took place in Connecticut during the four wars, the colony sent hundreds of soldiers to fight elsewhere.

During King William's War, Connecticut sent troops to help defend neighboring New York from Frenchmen and Indians. Connecticut was invaded during this war, but not by the French or the Indians. Instead, the problem came from the

New York Colony, which Connecticut troops had helped protect.

New York's Governor Benjamin Fletcher wanted the Connecticut militia to be under his command rather than under that of Connecticut officials. He argued that New York and not Connecticut was under attack, and that the Connecticut troops could do the most good by going where he ordered. Governor Fletcher obtained permission from England's King William III to take control of the Connecticut militia.

As might be expected from the colony that had refused to turn in its charter, Connecticut people opposed this. They wanted their troops on hand in case of attack, and they felt that Fletcher had no right to meddle in affairs that were protected by their charter.

Governor Fletcher came to Hartford to take command of the militia on October 26, 1693. That was almost exactly six years since the Halloween when Governor Andros had come after Connecticut's charter. Fletcher ordered the militia to assemble, which the men did. An aide then began reading the order that placed Fletcher in charge of Connecticut's militia.

The aide couldn't be heard, though, because Captain Joseph Wadsworth of the militia had his men beat their drums. Several times Governor Fletcher told the men to stop. Each time they did stop, only to start again when the aide resumed reading. Finally, Captain Wadsworth reputedly told the governor, "If you interrupt my drumming again, I will make the sun shine through you." That was a fancy way of threatening to shoot him.

This was the same Captain Joseph Wadsworth who had been credited with hiding the Connecticut charter in the Charter Oak. Wadsworth's threat helped scare Fletcher into returning to New York without trying to take command of the Connecticut militia. Connecticut lawmakers also sent Fitz-John Winthrop, a son of John Winthrop, Jr., to England. Fitz-John convinced the king that Connecticut should remain in charge of its own militia, and that Connecticut's charter should be honored in the future. However, Connecticut did agree to provide 120 men to help fight King William's War under the command of the New York governor.

King William's War did not settle the dispute between France and England. A few years later the struggle continued in Queen Anne's War, during which Connecticut men helped English forces capture Port Royal in Canada from the French. Queen Anne's War didn't settle things, either, nor

A French soldier of the time of the French and Indian War

The victorious English troops march into Louisbourg.

did King George's War, during which over 500 Connecticut men helped English forces seize the French fortress of Louisbourg in Canada. The dispute between England and France was not settled until the French and Indian War, which began in 1754.

## THE FOUNDING OF YALE COLLEGE

A much happier event than providing soldiers for wars took place in Connecticut at the start of the 1700s. John Davenport had made plans for building a college in New Haven soon after helping to found the colony in 1638. But because of the cost, and also because Harvard University was rather close, Connecticut did not build its own college for many years.

Then in the fall of 1701, ten ministers met at the home of the Reverend Samuel Russell in Branford, Connecticut, to plan the founding of a college. In order to start the college's library, each of the ministers donated some books. As he placed his books on the table, each minister reportedly said, "I give these books for the founding of a college in this colony."

The ministers sent a petition to the Connecticut General Assembly asking that it pass an act to found a college. When this act passed in October of 1701, Yale College was born. Of all the colleges in the United States today, only Harvard University, founded in 1636, in Massachusetts, and the College of William and Mary, founded in 1693, in Virginia, came before Yale.

When it opened with one student in 1702, the college wasn't yet called Yale, and it wasn't yet located in New Haven, as it is now. It was called the Collegiate School, and classes were held in the home of the Reverend Abraham Pierson of Killing-

Elihu Yale

worth (now Clinton). After the Reverend Pierson died in 1707, the college moved to two other Connecticut sites. Not until 1716 did the college find a permanent home in New Haven.

Once in New Haven, the college did not prosper at first because of a money shortage. Then in 1718 an English merchant named Elihu Yale contributed a large sum of money to help the new college. That same year the college was named Yale in his honor. To this day, Yale (which officially became a university in 1887) is sometimes called Old Eli because Elihu Yale did so much to build it.

Yale quickly began producing noteworthy graduates. Among its early graduates were such men as Jonathan Edwards (class of 1720), Samuel Seabury (class of 1748), and Nathan Hale (class of 1773). Born in East Windsor, Connecticut, Edwards was a religious leader who helped spread the Great Awakening religious revival throughout New England during the 1730s and 1740s. Born in Groton, Connecticut, Seabury was another important religious leader. In 1784 he was made the first American Episcopalian bishop. Nathan Hale was to become a great Revolutionary War hero.

Noah Webster, who compiled the famous *Webster's Dictionary*, graduated from Yale in

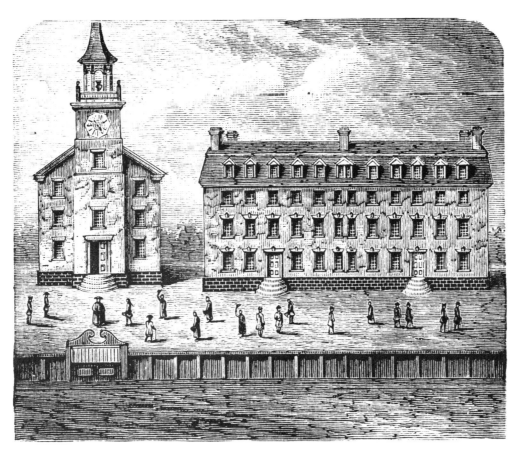

Yale College in 1784

1778. Eli Whitney, the inventor of the cotton gin, was a class of 1792 Yale graduate. Yale graduates of the 1800s included John C. Calhoun (class of 1804), who became the seventh vice president of the United States; Samuel F. B. Morse (class of 1810), who developed the telegraph and Morse code; and William Howard Taft (class of 1878), who became the twenty-seventh president of the United States. Yale graduates of the 1900s include

Dr. Benjamin Spock (class of 1925), who became a famous physician and author; and George Bush (class of 1948), who in 1988 was elected to be the forty-first president of the United States.

## CONNECTICUT YANKEES AND
## YANKEE PEDDLERS

Although the Colonial Wars were being fought outside Connecticut from time to time, the late 1600s and the first half of the 1700s were for the most part quiet years in the Land of Steady Habits. Most Connecticut people peacefully went about their business of farming and raising their families during those years.

Horses were fed hay during the winter.

As of the early 1700s, more than 90 out of every 100 Americans in Connecticut and the other colonies earned a living by farming. Today, in contrast, only about 4 out of every 100 people in the United States make their living by farming. More Americans now work at manufacturing or selling products than at any other activity.

The nation didn't change from a mainly farming to a mainly manufacturing country overnight. It happened slowly, beginning with some changes in colonial times. Connecticut played a vital role in some of these events.

Connecticut had several qualities that helped make it an early manufacturing center. It had raw matcrials, including timber, iron, and copper. Within Connecticut there were rivers for transportation, while nearby was the ocean for shipping products to distant ports. Connecticut also had many shrewd people who realized that money could be made in other ways besides farming.

A blacksmith making horseshoe nails by hand

Connecticut people were involved in several manufacturing "firsts" in the mid-1700s. In 1740, Edward and William Pattison of Berlin, Connecticut, made the first American tinware. In 1744, a Simsbury blacksmith named Samuel Higley helped establish the steel industry in the American colonies. In 1750, the first American hat factory was established at Wethersfield. By the mid-1700s, Connecticut people were also making such products as brass goods, nails, silk cloth, and clocks in small factories.

Not all Connecticut businessmen waited for customers to come to them. Some, such as the Pattison brothers, packed their goods into bags or carts and took them from town to town. There were also people who stocked up on such items as buttons, hats, stockings, mittens, pins, clocks, tinware, combs, and cloth and went from place to place selling them.

A Yankee peddler shows his goods to Connecticut homemakers.

These traveling salesmen became known as "Yankee peddlers" or "Connecticut Yankee peddlers." The word *Yankee* was a nickname for people in Connecticut and the other northern colonies, especially New England. The word may have come from the Scottish word *yankie*, meaning a clever woman. Or perhaps *Yankee* came from *Jan Kees* (John Cheese), the nickname given by the Dutch in New York to the English settlers in Connecticut. There are other theories of how the word *Yankee* originated. In any case, the Yankee peddlers became known as very shrewd salesmen. Stories about their shrewdness even gave Connecticut one of its nicknames—the Nutmeg State.

Nutmeg is a spice that was in great demand in colonial times. Nutmegs were hard to obtain because they did not grow in the American colonies. According to tall stories, Connecticut peddlers sold fake nutmegs made of wood to their customers. By the time the customers realized that they had been fooled, the Connecticut peddlers were far away! Connecticut is still sometimes called the Nutmeg State because of these old stories about wooden nutmegs.

In the 1800s, after colonial times were over, Connecticut became a very big manufacturing center where many products were made in large factories. But the roots of Connecticut industry reach back to the 1700s, when a small number of Connecticut manufacturers and peddlers began making and selling a few products.

A small Connecticut town in colonial days

# Chapter VII

## Life in Connecticut in the 1750s

*One for the bug,*
*One for the crow,*
*One to rot,*
*And two to grow.*

> *Old rhyme Connecticut farmers said while*
> *planting corn*

### A COLONY OF SMALL TOWNS

By 1750 the Connecticut Colony was home to about 110,000 people. Some huge sports stadiums can hold nearly that many people today. Yet Connecticut had the fifth-highest population of the Thirteen Colonies at the time, behind only the populations of Virginia, Massachusetts, Maryland, and Pennsylvania.

Today, Connecticut is a melting pot containing people of many different ethnic backgrounds, religions, and races. Even in the 1600s and 1700s, many of the colonies had large numbers of people of Scottish, Irish, African, German, Dutch, French, Swedish, and other origins. The Connecticut

Colony, on the other hand, had relatively few non-English people.

No big cities existed in Connecticut during the 1750s. A census taken in 1756 showed that Middletown, with about 5,700 people, was Connecticut's largest town. Here is a list of Connecticut's five largest towns as of 1756, with a comparison of their populations then and in the late 1980s:

| Town | Population in 1756 | Population in the Late 1980s |
|---|---|---|
| 1. Middletown | 5,700 | 39,000 |
| 2. Norwich | 5,500 | 38,000 |
| 3. New Haven | 5,100 | 123,000 |
| 4. Fairfield | 4,500 | 53,000 |
| 5. Windsor | 4,200 | 26,000 |

This woodcut of New Haven, dating from 1786, appeared in each edition of the *New Haven Chronicle.*

Hartford, which for most of colonial times was a "twin capital" of Connecticut along with New

The Green at Fairfield, Connecticut, in the 18th century

Haven, had just 3,000 people in 1756. (Connecticut lawmakers met sometimes at Hartford and sometimes at New Haven.)

A typical Connecticut town had a public park called a common or green at its center. On or near the common were the town's important buildings—the church, the school, the general store, and the inn.

Most families lived on farms within a few miles of the common. Often, the common was at a crossroads where two dirt roads met. When people from outlying farms wanted to go to town, they walked there over these roads or rode on horseback or in horse-drawn wagons.

Most Connecticut families lived in wooden houses that had brick fireplaces and chimneys for fire prevention. Since families tended to be large, a typical Connecticut farmhouse had about eight rooms.

## OBTAINING THE NECESSITIES OF LIFE

Connecticut had few very rich or very poor people in the 1750s. Most families had to work very hard to produce their own food, clothing, and many other necessities.

Nearly every family—even the families of ministers, teachers, doctors, lawyers, and Yankee peddlers—produced most of their own food. A family usually had a cow to supply milk, and chickens to provide eggs. Food crops grown by Connecticut families included corn, peas, wheat, and apples. Many families obtained a portion of their food by fishing and hunting.

Water came from a well that was usually located near the rear door of the farmhouse. But in colonial times, water wasn't the customary drink that it is today. Lacking the systems we have to make sure our water is pure, the colonists felt (often correctly) that their water was unhealthy. The most popular drink in colonial Connecticut was cider, which was usually made of apples or pears. Although the cider was alcoholic, children drank it, too.

Colonial families worked together in the fields, and they used tools such as those shown above to make the things they needed.

Nearly every family produced much of their own clothing. Many families raised sheep and grew a crop called flax. The sheep wool was woven into warm, sturdy clothing. The flax was spun into linen yarn on a spinning wheel, and then the yarn was woven into cloth on a loom. The cloth was then used to make clothing.

The colonists also produced many other necessities on their farms. For example, after a hog was slaughtered and eaten, its bones were ground up into fertilizer, its fat was made into

Feeding the pigs

Farmers cutting tobacco

soap, and its bristles were used to make brushes. After a pumpkin was eaten, its shell might become a lantern or might even be placed on people's heads and used as a hair-cutting guide!

One major change in farming took place around the year 1750. Farmers in the Connecticut River Valley had grown tobacco as an important crop for about 100 years. But by 1750 tobacco wasn't earning farmers much money, partly because of the competition from Virginia tobacco. (Years later, an expensive variety called shade-grown tobacco became an important crop in Connecticut, but that happened long after the end of colonial times.) As tobacco-growing became less common around 1750, the raising of farm animals, including cattle, sheep, horses, and hogs, became more popular.

There were some items that people generally bought in stores. Among these were fancy "Sunday clothes," certain foods such as sugar and spices, and guns and ammunition. There were some dollar bills and coins in use in Connecticut by the 1750s. However, most people obtained the things they couldn't produce for themselves by trading for them.

Sheep being sheared by hand. The wool comes off in a single piece called a fleece.

Most families took all their extra corn, beef, cider, pork, and vegetables to the general store near the common. The storekeeper traded rum, spices, sugar, tools, guns, clothes, and glassware to the family in exchange for their farm products.

The goods offered for sale in the general store were obtained through a string of merchants

A well-dressed couple shopping in a colonial store

from other Connecticut towns, other American colonies, the British islands in the Caribbean Sea, and Europe. And through a string of merchants the Connecticut families' farm products were ultimately sold in other Connecticut towns, other American colonies, the British islands in the Caribbean Sea, and Europe.

Because of the growing importance of manufacturing and selling and trading products in Connecticut, people were starting to go into other businesses besides farming. Small numbers of people were becoming store owners, merchants, and manufacturers. Some people were entering the shipping business, with the result that by the mid-1750s Connecticut colonists owned about seventy ships. Lawyers were needed to oversee deals between merchants and storekeepers, so the legal profession was also growing.

## FAMILY LIFE

The typical Connecticut family in the year 1750 consisted of a mother, a father, about seven children, and perhaps several other relatives such as grandparents. One reason for these large families was that children were needed to help with farm work. And in the days before vaccines were available, parents were also afraid of losing several children in the epidemics of smallpox and other diseases that swept through the colonies from time to time.

Every family member except the babies had work to do. The father did the heavy farm work and made all the family's business decisions. He was considered the head of the family, and his word was law. A child who disobeyed his or her father was considered to have done something terribly wrong. The father was also held accountable for the whole family's actions. If a child broke the law, the father could be punished just as though he had committed the crime.

The mother of the family was responsible for most of the work in the home. She spent thousands of hours raising her children. There were very few doctors in colonial Connecticut. When her children were sick, the mother did her best to nurse them, often using home remedies like herbal tea. The mother also had to make her family's food, clothes, candles, and soap. As if all this were not enough, she also did the cleaning and some of the lighter farm work.

As soon as they could walk, children were assigned chores. The youngest ones might scare birds away from the growing crops. Later, children learned to feed the livestock and fetch water from

A family planting corn in the backwoods

A colonial kitchen fireplace

the well. Older girls helped their mothers cook, sew, and care for younger brothers and sisters. Older boys chopped wood for the fireplace and helped their fathers clear fields and plant and harvest crops.

The family spent much more time together than most families do today. The typical family ate three meals a day together. They began the day with a large breakfast to provide them with energy for the day. At noon, fathers came home from the fields and many children came home from school for the biggest meal of the day, which the colonists called "dinner." The evening meal, which was usually the lightest meal of the day, was called "supper." The colonists did not need a big evening meal to provide energy because they generally went to bed much earlier than we do today.

After supper, the family might spend an hour or two sitting by the fireplace. They would read the Bible together or do handicrafts while discussing the day's events. Lights—or rather candles—would be out by around ten o'clock at night. The family needed sleep in order to start the next day's work at dawn.

The "Sabbath" or "Lord's Day" lasted from sunset on Saturday to sunset on Sunday. The family did no work on Saturday night. Instead, they got their "Sunday clothes" ready and perhaps took one of their occasional baths. The family attended church services together on Sunday. In many cases the services took up half a day and consisted of a two-hour sermon and much praying and hymn-singing.

A husband and wife were expected to stay married for life, so there were few divorces in colonial Connecticut. A person who wanted a divorce had to ask Connecticut lawmakers for permission. The Assembly granted divorces only for extreme reasons, such as when a husband beat his wife.

Because the colonists had such strict, rule-filled lives, many people have the wrong idea that there was little love in their families. Colonial families were similar to other families throughout history. In some, the people merely put up with each other. In some, there was a great deal of turmoil. But most families were warm and loving, even though they didn't openly display their love for each other as many people do today.

## SCHOOLS AND RELIGION

Besides helping a great deal around the house, most (but not all) Connecticut children attended school as of 1750. Probably only Massachusetts took as much interest as Connecticut did in the education of its young people.

Connecticut had many one-room schoolhouses attended by children of all ages. Since it was difficult to have separate lessons for children of various ages, the older children taught the younger ones. The teacher walked around with a rod ready to rap the knuckles of students who talked too much or made errors in their work.

( 9 )

17. Bite not thy bread, but break it, but not with flovenly Fingers, nor with the fame wherewith thou takeft up thy meat,

18 Dip not thy Meat in the Sawce.

19. Take not falt with a greazy Knife.

20 Spit not, cough not, nor blow thy Nofe at Table if it may be avoided ; but if there be neceffity, do it afide, and without much noife.

21. Lean not thy Elbow on the Table, or on the back of thy Chair.

22. Stuff not thy mouth fo as to fill thy Cheeks; be content with fmaller Mouthfuls.

23. Blow not thy Meat, but with Patience wait till it be cool.

24. Sup not Broth at the Table, but eat it with a Spoon.

A page from an early book on table manners

In Adam's fall
We sinned all.

Thy life to mend,
God's Book attend.

The Cat doth play,
And after slay.

A Dog will bite
A thief at night.

The Eagle's flight
Is out of sight.

The idle Fool
Is whipped at school.

As runs the Glass,
Man's life doth pass.

My book and Heart
Shall never part.

Job feels the rod,
Yet blesses God.

Proud Korah's troop
Was swallowed up.

The Lion bold
The Lamb doth hold.

The Moon gives light
In time of night.

Nightingales sing
In time of spring.

The royal Oak, it was the tree
That saved his royal majesty.

Peter denies
His Lord, and cries.

Queen Esther comes in royal state,
To save the Jews from dismal fate.

Rachel doth mourn
For her first-born.

Samuel anoints
Whom God appoints.

Time cuts down all,
Both great and small.

Uriah's beauteous wife
Made David seek his life.

Whales in the sea
God's voice obey.

Xerxes the Great did die,
And so must you and I.

Youth forward slips—
Death soonest nips.

Zaccheus, he
Did climb the tree,
His Lord to see.

A page from the *New England Primer*

One very popular textbook in 1750 was the *New England Primer*, which had first been published in Boston over fifty years earlier. Most of the textbooks were from England, however. They used English spellings of words and gave examples from English history and geography.

Girls were taught only reading, writing, and a little math at the schools. A girl seeking advanced education had to be taught at home by a private tutor or a parent. But for boys there were schools offering Latin and Greek—necessary languages for those headed for college. A college education was a rarity as of 1750, though. Yale, which was still Connecticut's only college, had just seventeen graduates in 1750 and twenty-two in 1751.

One interesting school was founded in Lebanon, Connecticut, in about 1750 by a minister named Dr. Eleazar Wheelock. Dr. Wheelock educated Indians at this school, which was known as Moor's Indian Charity School. In 1769, Dr. Wheelock moved his school to Hanover, New Hampshire. There its name was changed to Dartmouth College (New Hampshire's first college) and the idea of a special school for Indians was dropped.

Many changes involving religion were taking place in Connecticut around the year 1750. For

The drummer called the people to church.

many years, the Congregationalists (the new name for the Puritans) had been Connecticut's main religious group. They were called Congregationalists because they felt that each congregation should run its own affairs and choose its own minister. But many people had become unhappy with the Congregational churches.

The Great Awakening, a religious movement that reached Connecticut in 1740, helped bring this about. During the 1740s, many traveling preachers came to Connecticut and "awakened" people to the idea that they should be more personally involved in religion. Disappointed that their own preachers did not stir their hearts about religion and that their churches had become too worldly, many people left the Congregational churches.

In 1742, the General Assembly made a law to keep traveling ministers from preaching in Connecticut. But this law was repealed in 1750, partly because many people were eager to hear new religious ideas. By the 1750s, many Connecticut people who had left the Congregational churches had joined the Church of England or become Quakers or Baptists.

Traveling preacher

## RECREATION

Despite all their work, the Connecticut colonists found time for fun. They entertained themselves in simple ways. For example, families often sat together and talked. Friends and relatives took turns visiting one another.

Children made kites and flew them in the spring. In the winter, they made skates out of bones and then ice-skated on frozen ponds and streams. Children also played with dolls and enjoyed such games as hopscotch, leapfrog, and marbles. There were also a few storybooks for children.

Reading was gaining in popularity during the 1750s. But since books were costly, few families owned more than a Bible and perhaps five other volumes. *Robinson Crusoe* and *Gulliver's Travels* were among the popular books.

Until 1755, Connecticut did not have its own newspaper. People learned the news by talking to the Yankee peddlers who traveled from town to town, or by reading a newspaper from another colony. Then in 1755, the colony's first newpaper, the *Connecticut Gazette*, was founded by James Parker in New Haven. Back then, a single newspaper would be handed about in taverns and stores until dozens of people had read it.

The Connecticut colonists enjoyed several holiday. Although the first Thanksgiving had been held in Massachusetts in 1621, Connecticut did more than any other colony to establish Thanksgiving as a regular holiday. Except for 1675, when King Philip's War was being fought, Connecticut has held Thanksgiving celebrations every year since 1649. The birthday of England's king was another popular holiday. Towns celebrated it by firing cannons and holding parades. People celebrated Election Day by eating Election Cakes and drinking Election Beer.

# TRAVELS

INTO SEVERAL

## Remote Nations

OF THE

# WORLD.

In FOUR PARTS.

By *LEMUEL GULLIVER*, First a SURGEON, and then a CAPTAIN of several SHIPS.

VOL. I.

*LONDON·*

*Printed for* BENJ. MOTTE, *at the Middle* Temple-Gate *in* Fleet-street.
MDCCXXVI.

*Gulliver's Travels* was written by Jonathan Swift.

Robinson Crusoe, from the book by Daniel Defoe

Many church leaders frowned on dancing, card playing, and the theater, but many people pursued these activities anyway. Couples danced at weddings and balls. Some men played cards in taverns and private homes. Performers put on short comical plays called drolls. Families also attended Punch and Judy puppet shows and traveling circus shows.

## POLITICS

By 1754, eight of the thirteen American colonies were royal colonies—directly controlled by the king of England. The king ruled his royal colonies through governors sent from England.

Connecticut, on the other hand, was a charter colony. Its famous charter of 1662, which was eighty-eight years old and still going strong in 1750, granted the colony a great deal of self-rule. In fact, Connecticut and Rhode Island (which was also a charter colony) had more self-government than any of the other Thirteen Colonies. Connecticut and Rhode Island were more like small independent nations than English colonies.

As of the 1750s, voting was still limited to the men who owned property. Women, poorer white men, the few hundred Indians left in Connecticut, and black people could not vote. Many people don't realize it, but all thirteen colonies allowed slavery. As of the 1750s, Connecticut was home to about 3,000 black people, the great majority of them slaves. Even the nonslaves, who were called free blacks, suffered from discrimination in the colonies. Connecticut's free blacks had to pay the same taxes as white people, yet they could not vote, hold office, or serve on juries.

Connecticut people tended to elect their lawmakers again and again, which was one reason for the nickname Land of Steady Habits. Even Connecticut's election laws made it difficult for a newcomer to unseat an official. There were many Connecticut lawmakers who served for thirty years or more. For example, Hezekiah Wyllys and his son and grandson served one after the other as Connecticut's secretary of state for a total of ninety-eight years! And from 1689 to 1788 Connecticut had only eleven governors.

What really makes this amazing was that elections were held each year in colonial Connecticut. Voters had more of a chance to turn officials out of office than they do today, when elections are held less often. When their rights were threatened in the 1770s, however, the Connecticut colonists showed that they were ready to make some very big changes.

Israel Putnam

# Chapter VIII

# The Revolutionary War

*I only regret that I have but one life to lose for my country.*

*Nathan Hale's famous last words*

*How often have I had to lie whole stormy, cold nights in a wood, on a field, or a bleak hill ... with nothing but the canopy of the heavens to cover me. ... Oftentimes have I gone one, two, three, and even four days without a morsel [of food], unless the fields or forests might chance to afford enough to prevent absolute starvation. ...*

*From* Private Yankee Doodle, *by Revolutionary War soldier Joseph Plumb Martin of Connecticut*

## THE FRENCH AND INDIAN WAR (1754-1763)

King William's War, Queen Anne's War, and King George's War had not settled the fight over North American lands between France and Britain. It took a fourth Colonial War to do this— the French and Indian War.

Again, no fighting took place in Connecticut. Yet the colony was at or near first place in its contribution to the English cause. Connecticut sent over 5,000 men into battle—about one in every five of the colony's males between the ages of sixteen and forty-five. They fought mainly in the New York Colony and Canada. Connecticut also spent a huge sum of money on supplies for the war effort.

Israel Putnam of Pomfret, Connecticut, became famous during the French and Indian War by performing one heroic feat after another. Putnam and thousands of other Connecticut men helped England win the French and Indian War. As the winner in the struggle, England took control of Canada and all French possessions (except New Orleans) east of the Mississippi River in what is now the United States.

## TAXES AND MORE TAXES

The Americans had thought that England, the mother country, would be grateful for all their help during the French and Indian War. But the colonists were in for a shock. Many English lawmakers pointed out that the war had been fought partly to protect the American colonies from France. Therefore, they argued, the Americans should provide some of the money England needed to pay its war debts and to patrol its newly won North American lands.

England's Parliament (lawmaking body) along with King George III and other English officials decided that the Americans should pay certain taxes. A few English lawmakers warned that the Americans would hate this, and might even rebel. But most people in England felt that the Americans would complain about the taxes as people often do, and then pay them.

The mother country passed a number of tax bills during the 1760s and early 1770s. The Americans were told to pay taxes on many items ranging from legal papers to tea. As some English lawmakers had warned, most Americans hated these taxes, and many refused to pay them.

British tax stamps

The colonists especially loathed the Stamp Act that Parliament passed in spring of 1765. Scheduled to take effect on November 1, 1765, the Stamp Act was designed to raise money in many areas of daily life. Americans were supposed to buy special stamps and place them on newspapers, wills, and even marriage licenses.

In summer of 1765, a group of Connecticut leaders met to organize resistance to the Stamp Act. Among the Connecticut men at this meeting were the lawmaker Jonathan Trumbull and the war hero Israel Putnam. The Connecticut leaders formed a group called the Sons of Liberty to

New York protesters march against the Stamp Act.

oppose the Stamp Act. The other colonies also formed their own Sons of Liberty groups to fight the new tax.

A New Haven lawyer named Jared Ingersoll was assigned to distribute Connecticut's tax stamps. In the fall of 1765, Connecticut was the scene of many protests against Ingersoll and the Stamp Act, with the Sons of Liberty taking a leading role. A New Haven town meeting voted that Ingersoll should quit as Connecticut's stamp master. In

Lebanon, Connecticut, people dressed up a dummy to look like Ingersoll and then burned it as a crowd cheered. Protest meetings were held in Windham and Norwich.

In September, Ingersoll began riding on horseback from New Haven toward Hartford, which was then serving as the Connecticut capital. In Hartford, Ingersoll wanted to speak to Governor Thomas Fitch, who like himself favored obeying the British tax laws. He hoped Fitch could persuade the General Assembly to cooperate with the stamp tax. But as Ingersoll rode along, angry Sons of Liberty armed with clubs gathered alongside him. They told him to quit as stamp master—if he knew what was good for him.

Jared Ingersoll

After riding for about forty miles, Ingersoll reached Wethersfield, just south of Hartford. By then, about 500 angry patriots surrounded him. Ingersoll bravely faced the mob for a while, pointing out that many people in western Connecticut were willing to pay the stamp tax. But as the Sons of Liberty waved their clubs at him, Jared Ingersoll realized that he had to do as they ordered. He read a statement they had prepared saying that he quit as stamp master. And he yelled out their slogan with them three times: "LIBERTY AND PROPERTY!"

The crowd, which had grown to nearly 1,000, then led Ingersoll the short distance to Hartford. There he was forced to repeat his resignation outside the building where Connecticut's General Assembly was meeting.

Similar protests took place in the other twelve colonies. As had happened in Connecticut, in most places the Sons of Liberty only threatened violence. In Massachusetts, though, the Sons of Liberty smashed buildings and beat people who wanted to cooperate with the stamp tax.

Seeing that the Stamp Act might lead to war, England repealed it in March of 1766. When the good news reached Connecticut, church bells were rung, cannons and fireworks were shot off, and people danced in front of bonfires. But even though English lawmakers had given in about the Stamp Act, they continued to anger the Americans by passing more tax laws.

Other factors were pulling America and England apart. While fighting together in the French and Indian War, men from various colonies had come to feel that they had more in common with one another as Americans than they had with the English people across the ocean. The growth of newspapers and the building of better roads in America during the mid-1700s also brought the colonists together. While reading about or visiting other colonies, Americans began to feel that they were one people.

There were some Americans, though, who still felt a strong attachment to the mother country and who did not complain very much about the taxes. Many of these people did a great deal of business with the mother country and wanted to protect their way of life. Even when England sent soldiers into Boston to control the tax protests, many rich people thought this action was proper. Those who strongly opposed the taxes and the use of English troops tended to be poorer people who felt that their lives would improve if the mother country stayed out of America's affairs.

In the Land of Steady Habits, the Connecticut River, which wound down the colony's middle, was a tough dividing line between the two groups. Western Connecticut had more of the richer people who favored obeying British tax laws. Over the next few years, these people became known as Loyalists because they were loyal to the mother country. Eastern Connecticut, where most of the colony's Sons of Liberty lived, was poorer and less developed than western Connecticut. Its people were generally much more rebellious than those in the west.

The eastern Connecticut patriots wanted to take control of the colony's government. At the May 1766 election they did this. Thomas Fitch was defeated in his bid to continue as Connecticut governor. Two patriots, William Pitkin and Jonathan Trumbull, were elected governor and deputy governor. Other patriots also won important offices from men who favored co-operating with Britain.

After Governor Pitkin died in the fall of 1769, the General Assembly chose Jonathan Trumbull to be governor. Trumbull, who served as Connecticut governor for fifteen years, was a leading American patriot during the war that Britain and America began fighting in 1775.

One event that brought the two sides closer to war was Parliament's passage of the Tea Act of 1773. Throughout the colonies, Americans reacted to this tax by refusing to buy British tea. And patriots in several colonies destroyed shipments of British tea. The most famous example of this was the Boston Tea Party of December 16, 1773, when about fifty patriots tossed 342 chests of British tea into Boston Harbor.

Britain closed Boston's port on June 1, 1774, and planned to keep it closed until Bostonians

The Boston Tea Party. The patriots were dressed like Indians.

paid for the tea they had destroyed. Many Bostonians were put out of work because of the port closing, and many were hungry because ships couldn't bring food to the city. The British hoped that this punishment would force the Bostonians to pay for the destroyed tea. But the Bostonians refused to do this. Colonists from Connecticut, New York, and Rhode Island sent corn, beef, fish, and sugar overland into Boston to feed its people.

Eliphalet Dyer

Silas Deane

Leaders throughout the Thirteen Colonies knew that they must cooperate if they were to solve their problems with the mother country. A big meeting, called the First Continental Congress, was held in Philadelphia, Pennsylvania, between September 5 and October 26, 1774. Every colony but Georgia sent delegates to this convention. Connecticut sent three men—Roger Sherman, Eliphalet Dyer, and Silas Deane.

Nearly all of the delegates at the First Continental Congress hoped that the disputes with Britain would be settled peacefully. But the Congress told the colonies to make sure their militias were armed and ready to fight—just in case war broke out with the mother country. In October of 1774, Connecticut's General Assembly ordered that the colony's militia begin intense training, and that Connecticut towns stock up on military supplies.

The First Continental Congress sent its complaints to British leaders. The delegates planned to hold a Second Continental Congress in Philadelphia starting on May 10, 1775, if Britain didn't give in about taxes, the Boston port closing, and other matters. Britain would not budge. Three weeks before the Second Continental Congress was to begin, war between Britain

Battle of Lexington

and America broke out. The Thirteen Colonies fought this Revolutionary War (1775–1783) to free themselves from British rule and become the United States of America.

The war began in Massachusetts on April 19, 1775. At dawn on that Wednesday, British troops (called redcoats because of their red uniforms) arrived at Lexington, Massachusetts. The British redcoats wanted to arrest the important American leaders John Hancock and Samuel Adams. The two men got away, but everything else went wrong for the Americans at Lexington.

About seventy-five militiamen gathered on Lexington Green to face the much larger number of redcoats who had arrived. These militiamen were farmers rather than soldiers, and when Britain's Major John Pitcairn told them to go home, most of them began to do just that. Suddenly the British started firing their guns. Eight Americans were killed and ten were wounded in this opening battle of the Revolution. A few Americans managed to return the fire, wounding just one redcoat. The redcoats then headed to nearby Concord, Massachusetts. With other British forces, they planned to destroy American military supplies in Concord.

Word of the Battle of Lexington soon spread across the Massachusetts countryside, drawing hundreds of angry militiamen to Concord. This time the Americans outnumbered the British. They pounded the redcoats at Concord's North Bridge, and continued to shoot at them as they retreated to Boston. Nearly 300 redcoats were killed or wounded during the battle and retreat from Concord. The Americans lost about 100 men in the Battle of Concord, which was the first American victory of the Revolutionary War.

Horseback riders were sent out from Massachusetts to spread the news of the battles of Lexing-

Battle at the North Bridge, Concord

ton and Concord to other colonies. It took about a day for the news to reach Connecticut. Soon about 3,600 Connecticut men were marching toward Cambridge, Massachusetts, where the Americans were forming a large army.

On June 17, 1775, at least 200 Connecticut men fought in a huge battle for control of the hills near Boston. This Battle of Bunker Hill was called a British victory because the redcoats took the hill they sought. However, 1,000 British troops were killed or wounded in the fighting, while the Americans lost about 400 men. Throughout the Thirteen Colonies, Americans proudly said, "We have more ground to sell them at the same price!"

Uniform of the 1st Connecticut Regiment, 1778

Soon after the Battle of Bunker Hill, the Virginian George Washington arrived in Massachusetts to take command of the Americans' newly created Continental Army.

As in the four Colonial Wars, no major Revolutionary War battle was fought in Connecticut. But the colony contributed a large share of men and supplies to the American cause. It is estimated that about 30,000 Connecticut men fought in the Revolution. Only Massachusetts is believed to have contributed more soldiers to the Continental Army. Connecticut also had a very small percentage of Loyalists—people who favored Britain in the war. Throughout the colonies, about 25 out of every 100 adults were Loyalists. In Connecticut, only about 6 in every 100 adults were Loyalists, and the only area with a sizable number of Loyalists was the southwestern part of the colony.

Connecticut troops played important roles in many big Revolutionary War battles. Among them were the Battle of Bunker Hill in Massachusetts (1775), the Battle of Long Island in New York (1776), the Battle of Trenton in New Jersey (1776), the Battle of Saratoga in New York (1777), and the Battle of Germantown in Pennsylvania (1777).

They also fought in the war's decisive battle at Yorktown, Virginia, in 1781.

While Connecticut soldiers were fighting on land, Connecticut sailors and ships were battling the enemy at sea. The small Connecticut navy captured over 40 enemy vessels. Connecticut also commissioned over 200 privately owned ships to attack British vessels. These privateers, as they were called, reportedly captured about 500 British vessels. Also during the Revolutionary War, David Bushnell of Saybrook, Connecticut, built the first American submarine. Bushnell's one-man vessel, the *Turtle*, attempted to blow up a British ship in New York Harbor. Although the mission failed,

A privateers' recruiting office in New London, Connecticut

this was the start of submarine warfare, which became commonplace in later wars.

Before the Battle of Yorktown cinched the American victory, George Washington and the American troops had some awful years. The Continental Army often lacked enough food, clothing, and supplies. Many times, Governor Jonathan Trumbull sent large quantities of these items from Connecticut. One of Trumbull's most helpful acts came in early 1778, when he arranged to send a large amount of beef to Valley Forge, Pennsylvania. The army, which was wintering at Valley Forge, needed that food to survive.

Ragged soldier stands guard at Valley Forge.

George Washington's nickname for Jonathan Trumbull was Brother Jonathan. Whenever the army needed supplies, Washington would say, "We must speak to Brother Jonathan about it." Brother Jonathan became a nickname for any American patriot during the Revolution. And it soon came to be a nickname for the whole nation, just as Uncle Sam is today. Because of all the supplies sent by Brother Jonathan and its other residents, Connecticut was nicknamed the Provisions State during the war.

The change from "colony" to "state" took place in July 1776. Three weeks after the battles of Lexington and Concord in 1775, the Second

Continental Congress opened in Philadelphia. By the spring of 1776, there was a growing feeling that the colonies should declare themselves free of Britain. The war had been going on for a year, and most Americans were so bitter that they didn't want to return to British rule even if the mother country made peace.

In June of 1776, the Continental Congress decided that in early July it would vote on whether the colonies should free themselves from Britain. On June 15, Connecticut's lawmakers in Hartford instructed the Connecticut delegates in Philadelphia to vote for independence. The historic vote was made late on July 2, 1776. Connecticut and eleven other colonies voted for American independence. The thirteenth colony, New York, did not vote on July 2, but made the independence vote unanimous a few days later.

The delegates in Philadelphia thought that July 2, 1776, would be considered the day the United States had been born. Two days later, on July 4, the delegates adopted a paper explaining why the Thirteen Colonies had chosen to become the thirteen United States of America. This paper, the Declaration of Independence, was printed in all the newspapers and read to cheering crowds throughout the thirteen new states. Because the

Declaration began with the words "In Congress, July 4, 1776," Americans began celebrating the nation's birthday on the Fourth of July and have done so ever since, even though July 2 was the actual date that American lawmakers had chosen independence.

Delegates from all thirteen new states signed the Declaration of Independence. Connecticut had four signers—Roger Sherman, Samuel Huntington, William Williams, and Oliver Wolcott. Their signatures can be seen in the Declaration's far right-hand column. Soon after the Declaration was signed in Philadelphia, the Connecticut soldier Nathan Hale, whose story is told on page 139, said the last words that made him perhaps the most famous of the thousands of Americans who died in the fight for independence.

Although no major Revolutionary War battles were fought there, Connecticut was the scene of four British raids. In April 1777, 2,000 redcoats under Major General William Tryon attacked Danbury in far western Connecticut. The British burned Danbury, killed some of its townspeople, and destroyed food and military supplies that American troops needed. While withdrawing, the redcoats were attacked by American militiamen, some of whom were led by Connecticut's Benedict

Arnold. The Americans killed a few redcoats but could not recover the military supplies.

The second British raid took place in February 1779, when General Tryon and his men attacked Greenwich, in Connecticut's southwestern tip. The redcoats did a great deal of damage to Greenwich before they were driven off by Connecticut militiamen under Israel Putnam.

The third raid into Connecticut began on July 5, 1779, the day after the United States third birthday. First, the British troops fought their way into New Haven, where they killed and wounded a few people and destroyed part of the town. The redcoats then destroyed about 100 homes and about 100 other buildings in and around Fairfield. The raid concluded with the destruction of most of Norwalk, Connecticut.

Compared to the final British raid, Connecticut losses in the first three raids were small. A great deal of blood was shed during the fourth and final British raid. What made this raid especially bitter was that the British forces were led by Benedict Arnold, an American hero who had turned traitor.

On September 6, 1781, Arnold led 2,000 men to the region of New London and Groton, two towns on opposite sides of the Thames River in southeastern Connecticut. Taking about half his forces,

A young woman attempts to
shoot Benedict Arnold.

Arnold destroyed a large part of New London.
Meanwhile, nearly 1,000 redcoats attacked Fort
Griswold, which protected the town of Groton.
Although greatly outnumbered, about 150
Americans under Lieutenant Colonel William
Ledyard fought bravely, killing a number of the
redcoats who tried to take the fort.

Finally, the British made a terrific charge on Fort Griswold and the Americans had to surrender. But as William Ledyard handed over his sword, a redcoat murdered him. The British then massacred about 80 other surrendering Americans at Fort Griswold. Although Benedict Arnold had been in New London at the time, Connecticut people blamed him for the massacre, which occurred near the place where 700 Pequot Indians had been slaughtered back in 1637.

Soon after the Fort Griswold massacre, the Americans won the key battle of the war far to the south of Connecticut. In late September of 1781, George Washington led his 17,000-man army to Yorktown, Virginia, where an 8,000-man British army was stationed. Among General Washington's men at Yorktown were ten Connecticut companies.

France had joined the American side in early 1778. While Washington's forces blocked escape by land, French vessels blocked the British from escaping by sea. For several days the British and the Americans exchanged cannon fire. Finally, after losing about 600 men, the British realized that their cause was hopeless. On October 19, 1781, General Charles Cornwallis surrendered his large army to General Washington.

Battle of Yorktown

This great American victory at the Battle of
Yorktown meant that the United States had won
the Revolutionary War. The war officially ended on
September 3, 1783, with the signing of a peace
treaty in Paris, France. By signing this paper,
England acknowledged that Connecticut and the
other twelve former colonies had become a new
nation—the United States of America!

# ISRAEL PUTNAM (1718–1790)

Israel Putnam was born in Salem Village (now Danvers) in Massachusetts. He was the twelfth child of a wealthy family. When Israel was about five years old, his father died, and his mother remarried several years later. While these family changes were taking place, Israel's education seems to have been ignored. He never learned to spell or write very well.

Israel Putnam

When he was twenty-one years old, Israel Putnam married eighteen-year-old Hannah Pope, the daughter of a neighboring farmer. Israel and Hannah moved to what is now Brooklyn in eastern Connecticut. Israel cleared the land and built a farm, where he and Hannah raised ten children, eight of whom lived past childhood.

Putnam was a successful farmer. He was credited with introducing a well-known apple of his time, and he raised large numbers of sheep. A threat to his sheep resulted in one of Israel Putnam's best-known adventures. During the winter of 1742–1743, a large wolf killed about seventy of Putnam's sheep and many of his neighbors' livestock. Finally, Israel Putnam and five neighbors tracked the wolf to a cave. Putnam tied a rope around his body, gave one end of it to his friends, and then crawled into the narrow cave. Just as the snarling wolf was about to spring at him, Putnam fired his gun. When his neighbors pulled Putnam out, he had the huge dead wolf in his arms.

Israel Putnam continued to farm successfully for the next few years. In 1755, the year after the French and Indian War had begun, he volunteered as a private in a Connecticut regiment. During the war, Putnam rose in rank while fighting in battles and making scouting missions in the New York region. He became a leader of a special fighting force called Rogers' Rangers. On July 1, 1757, Putnam and sixty Rangers sank a number of canoes carrying French and Indian enemies. Another time, Putnam was badly burned while saving a British fort from exploding. On yet another occasion he and a few men captured two armed enemy vessels on a river.

In the midst of a battle in 1758, Israel Putnam fought an Indian chief. Putnam's gun wouldn't fire. Just as the chief was about to brain him with his hatchet, Putnam raised his hands to surrender. The Indians then decided to burn Putnam to death. The first time they tried it, a rainstorm put out the flames. The second time, Putnam was rescued by a French soldier who respected the way he had fought. Putnam was taken as a prisoner to Canada, where an American finally paid for his release. He walked several hundred miles home to Connecticut.

In a final French and Indian War adventure, Putnam survived a shipwreck off Cuba's coast in 1762. Spain had joined the French side,

137

Israel Putnam leaving
for the Revolutionary War

and Putnam was helping to lead Connecticut forces against the Spanish-held city of Havana, Cuba. After reaching shore on rafts, Putnam and his men helped British forces capture Havana.

Despite his seven years of fighting for Britain during the French and Indian War, Putnam turned against the mother country when it began taxing America soon after the war ended. He was one of Connecticut's leading Sons of Liberty. When Putnam heard that the Revolutionary War had begun in April of 1775, he left the field he was plowing and rode about seventy miles in one day to the Boston area, where American troops were assembling.

Two months later, on June 17, 1775, "Old Put" led a portion of the American troops who fought in the Battle of Bunker Hill. The Americans were short of the powder that they needed to fire their guns. Not wanting the troops to waste shots, Israel Putnam (some say it was William Prescott) reportedly said, "Men, you are all marksmen—don't one of you fire until you see the whites of their eyes." The 57-year-old Putnam fought heroically at this battle, inspiring the younger soldiers to put up a great fight also.

Soon after the Battle of Bunker Hill, Israel Putnam was made one of George Washington's main generals. But "Old Put" was better at leading small bands of men than he was at organizing and leading large numbers of troops. He didn't do very well as a general in the Continental Army. His health also began to break down in about 1776, and in late 1779 his army career ended when he suffered a stroke that paralyzed him. Fortunately, Israel Putnam lived to see his country win the Revolutionary War and his old friend George Washington elected as its first president. "Old Put" died at home at the age of 72.

---

## NATHAN HALE (1755–1776)

Nathan Hale

Born in Coventry, Connecticut, on June 6, 1755, Nathan Hale was the sixth of twelve children. Those who knew him during his short life described him as being very intelligent, kindly, athletic, and handsome. He also put his whole heart and mind into whatever he was doing—whether it was schoolwork, sports, or serving his country.

Young men in the 1700s commonly entered college around the age of sixteen. When he was just fourteen, Nathan entered Yale, where he studied Latin, Greek, Hebrew, the Bible, and public speaking. He also became known as a great athlete at Yale. He once broad-jumped so far that Yale students were still talking about "Hale's jump" long after his death. He could throw and kick a football a great distance. And it was said that he could place one hand on a six-foot fence and vault over it.

Nathan graduated from Yale in 1773 at the age of eighteen. For the next two years he taught school in Connecticut—first in East Haddam and then in New London. Besides teaching a class of thirty-two boys during the regular school year in New London, he taught a summer-school class of about twenty young women between five and seven o'clock in the morning.

After the Revolutionary War broke out in 1775, Nathan quit his teaching job and joined the Continental Army. Between summer of 1775 and fall of 1776 he fought bravely in the campaigns against the British in Boston and New York City. He volunteered for the most dangerous assignments, and once even offered his pay to other soldiers so that they would stay in the army instead of going home.

In September 1776, Nathan was made captain of a band of 170 excellent fighting men called Knowlton's Rangers. George Washington wanted one

The execution of
Nathan Hale

of the Rangers to go on an extremely dangerous spying mission in the New York City region. Nathan's friends warned him that the man who went on this mission would very likely be captured and hanged. Nathan volunteered anyway, explaining that he owed it to his country to attempt what General Washington wanted.

Nathan dressed in a plain brown suit so that he would look like a schoolteacher instead of a soldier. Then for several days he spied on the British around New York City, which the redcoats had just seized. Nathan made sketches of the British positions and fortifications. But before he could return to American forces, he was captured. The British found Nathan's sketches and notes hidden in his shoes. They convicted him of being a spy and sentenced him to be hanged the next morning.

The British mistreated Nathan Hale on the last night of his life. They wouldn't let him speak to a minister or have a Bible. And the letters that he wrote to his family and friends were destroyed.

At around eleven o'clock in the morning on Sunday, September 22, 1776, the British prepared to hang Nathan Hale. Apparently a cruel British official said something taunting as the rope went around Nathan's neck. Nathan Hale's fourteen-word response brought him lasting fame. "I only regret that I have but one life to lose for my country," said the 21-year-old Nathan Hale, just before he was hanged.

We might never have known about Nathan Hale's brave speech if British soldiers at the execution hadn't told Israel Putnam and other Americans about it. News of Nathan Hale's last words spread throughout the country. They helped inspire thousands of other Americans to continue fighting and win the Revolutionary War.

---

Jonathan Trumbull

## JONATHAN TRUMBULL (1710–1785) AND HIS FAMILY

Jonathan Trumbull was born in 1710 in Lebanon, Connecticut. His father, a successful merchant, decided that Jonathan's older brother, Joseph, would go into the family business. Jonathan would become a minister.

To prepare for the ministry, Jonathan entered Harvard at the age of thirteen. After graduating four years later, Jonathan returned to Lebanon, where he studied religion with a local minister. He became a preacher at the age of twenty, and was soon asked to work as a minister in Colchester,

Connecticut, several miles from his home. However, sometime around New Year's Day in 1732, a ship carrying Jonathan's brother Joseph disappeared at sea. Jonathan's father then asked him to give up the ministry and join him in the business. Always dutiful, Jonathan did what his father asked.

Jonathan worked with his father for three years. In late 1735, Jonathan married Faith Robinson, a descendant of the Pilgrims John and Priscilla Alden. About that time, Jonathan's father retired because of illness. For about the next thirty years, Jonathan Trumbull ran a very successful business. He sold livestock and meat in such cities as Boston, Massachusetts, and Newport, Rhode Island. And in his general store in Lebanon, he sold such items as soap, butter, nails, buttons, combs, thimbles, eyeglasses, tea, paper, rum, and molasses. Meanwhile, in 1733 he was elected to the Connecticut General Assembly. For half a century he served as a Connecticut legislator, judge, deputy governor, and then governor.

Governor Trumbull's war office.

During the 1760s, Jonathan Trumbull's business fell apart. He had allowed too many customers to build up large debts, which they never paid. As a result, he in turn could not pay for goods he had ordered. Also, the colonies suffered hard times after the French and Indian War ended in 1763. By the late 1760s, his debt was so large that he had little hope of ever paying it. Too proud to declare himself bankrupt, he tried for many years to revive his business without success.

As he failed in business, Jonathan Trumbull rose in politics. Connecticut people liked his honesty and his opposition to British taxes. In 1766, he was elected deputy governor of Connecticut. After Governor William Pitkin died in 1769, Jonathan Trumbull became Connecticut governor—a position he held for fifteen years.

When the Revolutionary War began, Jonathan Trumbull was the only colonial governor to take the Americans' side. In fact, he supported the American cause as strongly as any public official in the new country. Governor Trumbull turned a building next to his home in Lebanon into what was called the Connecticut War Office. Thanks largely to Trumbull's work there, Connecticut was believed to have sent more men to the Continental Army than any other state except Massachusetts, and it sent such large quantities of supplies to the army that it was called the Provisions State.

Governor Trumbull's experience as a merchant helped him in gathering and distributing war materials. And his religious background helped him persuade men to join the army. He deeply believed that God wanted the

United States to be independent. He made fiery speeches and proclamations about how God would help free America—if enough men would join the army. At times, the man George Washington called Brother Jonathan seemed to be one of the few people who believed the Americans would win the war.

In 1784, the year after the American victory became official, Trumbull retired as Connecticut's governor. Jonathan Trumbull, one of the greatest people in Connecticut history, died in his hometown of Lebanon a little over a year later at the age of seventy-four.

Jonathan and Faith Trumbull also produced six remarkable children. Joseph was a member of the Continental Congress and an official in the Continental Army. Jonathan, Jr., was a member of the U. S. Congress from Connecticut and then governor of Connecticut. David was a Continental Army official. John was a famous artist, known for his Revolutionary War scenes. Faith married a prominent Revolutionary War soldier. And Mary became the wife of William Williams, a signer of the Declaration of Independence from Connecticut.

---

## BENEDICT ARNOLD (1741–1801)

People who harm their country for the sake of money or other personal gain are called traitors. Benedict Arnold was the most famous traitor in American history. But few people realize that before turning traitor he was one of the greatest American heroes of the Revolutionary War.

Benedict Arnold was born in Norwich, Connecticut, into a well-known family. One of his ancestors had been a governor of Rhode Island during the 1600s. Benedict's father was a prominent sea captain and merchant. He was also an alcoholic, which may have been a reason why young Benedict seemed to like being away from home.

At the age of eleven, Benedict went off to a boarding school a few miles from his home. At school he became known for his hot temper, athletic skill, and desire to show off. Once when a building caught fire, Benedict foolishly climbed onto the roof to show off for his classmates.

As Benedict's father continued his drunken ways, the Arnolds ran short of money. When Benedict was fourteen, his family could no longer afford the boarding school. He returned home, but soon ran away to join the Americans who were helping the British fight the French and Indian War. He served for several years and took part in campaigns in the New York region.

Benedict Arnold

Not long after his army service ended, Benedict Arnold moved to New Haven, Connecticut. There he opened a store where he sold medicines, books, and many other items. As his business prospered, he bought ships and sailed on voyages to distant lands to buy and sell goods. Once while off the coast of Honduras in Central America, Benedict Arnold got into an argument with a British sea captain. When the captain called him a "damned Yankee," Arnold challenged him to a gun duel. An excellent shot and very cool under pressure, Arnold wounded the sea captain, who then apologized.

Benedict Arnold was firmly on the American side at the start of the Revolutionary War. When news of the battles of Lexington and Concord reached New Haven, he marched a militia unit up to Massachusetts. Once there, he volunteered to lead a mission to seize Fort Ticonderoga in New York. He and Vermont's Ethan Allen led the capture of Fort Ticonderoga in May of 1775.

Several months later, George Washington approved Arnold's plan for capturing British-held Quebec, Canada. In the fall of 1775, Arnold led about 1,000 men on a 500-mile journey north from Massachusetts into Canada. A blizzard was raging when Arnold and his troops attacked the British at Quebec on New Year's morning, 1776. Arnold's leg was smashed by a musket ball during the terrible American defeat at the Battle of Quebec. But his bravery in leading his men on the long journey and in the difficult battle earned him a promotion to brigadier general.

Benedict Arnold had several other great moments during the war. One occurred in the fall of 1776, when he led American naval forces in a terrific battle against the British on Lake Champlain in New York. Another came in the fall of 1777, when he helped the Americans win the Battle of Saratoga in New York while suffering a terrible wound to the leg that had been injured at Quebec.

Had Benedict Arnold done nothing more in the war after the Battle of Saratoga, he would be honored today as one of the great heroes in American history. But Arnold felt that the American government did not appreciate him. Not only that, after he was placed in command of American forces in Philadelphia in mid-1778, he and his wife lived so expensively that he found himself needing money. The desire for money and the feeling that he was unappreciated were two main reasons why in the spring of 1779 Benedict Arnold offered to join the British side.

In the summer of 1780, George Washington placed Arnold in command of the American fort at West Point, New York. This was Arnold's chance to sell out his country. For a large sum of money, he agreed to surrender the fort to the British. Fortunately, the Americans learned of Arnold's plan in

September of 1780, before he could put it into effect. Knowing that he would be hanged as a traitor if captured, Arnold fled and joined the British army once his plan was discovered. Near the end of the war, he led British invasions into Virginia and Connecticut.

As word of his treason spread, the very name Benedict Arnold became dirty words to Americans. In New Haven, people made a dummy of Arnold and another dummy of the Devil behind him offering him money. They dragged the dummies through the streets. After the war, Benedict Arnold lived in Canada and England. He died in London, England, at the age of sixty, still hated by the people across the ocean in the land of his birth.

---

## JOSEPH PLUMB MARTIN (1760-1850)

The great leaders made the big decisions, but it took the sweat and blood of thousands of ordinary soldiers to win the Revolutionary War. We know less about these ordinary soldiers than we do about such heroes as George Washington and Jonathan Trumbull, who had a great deal written about them. But we do have some soldiers' diaries and journals. One of the most fascinating was written by a soldier named Joseph Plumb Martin.

Born in Becket, Massachusetts, in late 1760, Martin was a minister's son. He lived with his parents until he was about seven. Then because of family trouble, Joseph moved to his grandparents' farm in Milford, Connecticut, near New Haven.

Joseph spent the next few years planting and harvesting crops and doing other farm work. Apparently, he had little or no formal schooling, but read a great deal on his own. When the Revolutionary War began in 1775, Joseph wanted to join the army. His grandparents wouldn't let him, though, because he was just fourteen years old. Then one day when Joseph was fifteen, he enlisted. His grandparents were very upset, but he was so determined to be a soldier that they didn't stop him. They packed up a gun, clothes, food, and a Bible for Joseph, who then went off to fight the British. During the next seven years, he fought in a number of big battles and rose to the rank of sergeant in the Continental Army.

After the war ended, Joseph Plumb Martin moved to Maine, where he farmed, got married, and raised a family. When he was nearly seventy, Martin wrote a book about his Revolutionary War experiences, probably basing it on notes made during the war. A small printing of his book was made in 1830, but by the time Joseph Plumb Martin died in Maine at the age of nearly ninety, his book was largely forgotten. Then, over 100 years later in the 1960s, it was republished under the title *Private Yankee Doodle.*

*Private Yankee Doodle* paints a vivid picture of the life of a Revolutionary War soldier. Martin's great descriptions enable the reader to feel what it was like to face cannon fire and see one's friends wounded and killed. Yet Martin spends a rather small part of his book describing the battles in which he fought. Most of the book describes how he and his fellow soldiers were always trying to overcome their three "constant companions: Fatigue, Hunger, and Cold."

Martin describes long marches that lasted up to two days. He sometimes fell asleep on his feet during these long marches, only waking up when he bumped into someone. He and his "messmates," as he called his fellow soldiers, often slept out in the open under the rain or snow without even a fire. Martin was wet and cold so often that he came to envy the pigs he saw on farms, because at least they had a warm sty in which to sleep!

The American government was so poor that it was often unable to feed or pay the soldiers. Martin and his messmates had to raid beehives, shoot squirrels and pigeons, catch fish, and gather apples and nuts just to survive. Even so, there were many times when they went "four days without a morsel" of food. Once, on Thanksgiving Day, 1777, the men were gathered for what they expected would be a special feast. But all the American government could give them was rice and vinegar.

There were many times—often in the winter—when the men had no clothes or shoes. Martin was with George Washington's army in the winter of 1777-1778 at Valley Forge, Pennsylvania. Martin wrote that many of the men walked barefoot into Valley Forge, and that their bleeding feet turned the ground red. At Valley Forge and the Battle of Monmouth (fought in New Jersey in 1778), the clothing situation was so bad that a quarter of the troops didn't even have pants. They had to pull down their "ragged shirt flaps to cover their nakedness."

After years of such hardships, Martin and his messmates were happy when the peace treaty was signed in 1783. Yet Martin also felt very sad at leaving the men with whom he "had lived together as a family of brothers for several years."

Why did Martin and thousands of other Americans fight so long and hard for a country that couldn't feed, clothe, or pay them? His answer was that "the Americans were invincible [unbeatable] in my opinion," because they were fighting for their freedom.

The Connecticut State House in 1850

# Chapter IX

# Connecticut and the U.S. Constitution

*There was a time when I firmly believed that a separation from the mother country would be the greatest blessing. . . . I now see anarchy and confusion every day gaining ground among us. . . .*

*Israel Putnam, describing (in a letter written in 1783) how the country was falling apart after the Revolutionary War*

Few modern-day Americans realize it, but soon after the Revolutionary War ended, it looked as if the country would fall apart. In many ways, the United States was more like thirteen separate nations going in thirteen different directions than one nation made up of thirteen states.

Today, the United States has a strong central government to conduct its national affairs. The country has a president, and it has a Senate and a House of Representatives to make national laws and deal with other countries. It has a national court system, powerful armed forces, and a national money system. The United States also has national taxes to pay for all these services.

A copper coin of
Connecticut

Scales used for
weighing coins

None of this existed in the early 1780s. At that time, the nation was governed under the Articles of Confederation, an agreement that went into effect in 1781. Under the Articles, the central government (Congress) was pitifully weak. Because it wasn't allowed to raise taxes, Congress had to beg the states for money. Most of the states wouldn't give it. As a result, the country couldn't maintain anything but a tiny army or provide many of the national services we take for granted today.

The country had no president to lead it. There were no national courts. Instead of a national money system, states printed their own money and people used foreign money, all of which varied in value from place to place.

The federal government was weak because until about 1787 most Americans wanted it that way. There was a widespread fear that a strong federal government would tax people to death. Americans also felt that a strong U. S. government might meddle in people's and states' affairs too much.

One event that changed people's attitudes was Shays' Rebellion, a revolt by western Massachusetts farmers that lasted from September 1786 to February 1787. Because the tiny U. S. army lacked the men to put down the rebellion, the Massachusetts militia had to do it. People began to fear that

The Continental Congress issued paper money during the Revolutionary War.

the nation might be ripped apart by a series of rebellions. This convinced most people that a stronger national government was needed.

In the spring of 1787, a convention opened in Philadelphia in order to strengthen the U. S. government. Every state but Rhode Island sent delegates to this convention. Connecticut sent Oliver Ellsworth, William Samuel Johnson, and Roger Sherman. They helped forge a new set of basic laws—the United States Constitution.

Several times during the convention it looked as if the delegates would not be able to agree on a new Constitution. A major source of conflict concerned the number of U. S. lawmakers each state would have. The states with the largest populations wanted to have more lawmakers than the states with small populations. The states with small populations thought that each state should be represented equally in the new government.

Finally, Roger Sherman spelled out what is called the Connecticut Compromise. The states with more people should have more members in the House of Representatives. But each state should have an equal number of senators. Connecticut may have been nicknamed the Constitution State because the Connecticut Compromise was so vital to the U. S. Constitution.

George Washington, standing at right, was the president of the constitutional convention that wrote the Constitution of the United States of America.

After about four months, the Constitution was completed in September of 1787. William Samuel Johnson and Roger Sherman signed it for Connecticut.

Delaware became the first state by approving the Constitution on December 7, 1787. Then Pennsylvania (December 12, 1787), New Jersey (December 18, 1787), and Georgia (January 2, 1788) became the second, third, and fourth states.

In early January of 1788, delegates from each Connecticut town met in Hartford to decide whether or not to approve the Constitution. They talked and argued for five days. Finally, the vote was made on January 9, 1788. By a vote of 128 to 40, Connecticut approved the Constitution. Thus, a little more than 100 years after the famous Charter Oak incident, Connecticut became the fifth of the original Thirteen Colonies to join the United States under its new Constitution!

# ROGER SHERMAN (1721-1793)

Roger Sherman

Roger Sherman was born in Newton, Massachusetts, near Boston. When Roger was four years old, he and his family moved to nearby Stoughton, Massachusetts, where he grew up. His father, a shoemaker, taught Roger to follow in his footsteps. But Roger liked books more than making and fixing shoes. Although Roger had little formal schooling, it was said that he always kept an open book on his cobbler's bench so that he could read while working on shoes.

When he was 22, Roger Sherman moved to New Milford, Connecticut, reportedly walking the nearly 150 miles with his shoemaker's tools on his back. After living in New Milford for two years, he was appointed county surveyor—a person who determines land boundaries. This was the first of many public offices that Sherman held. Besides his surveying work, during the 1750s he also ran a country store with a brother, studied law and became a lawyer, served as a legislator and as a judge, published an almanac, and invested in real estate.

In 1761, Roger Sherman moved to New Haven, Connecticut, where he continued to hold many public offices. Although he was an awkward speaker, shy, and not college educated, Sherman became one of Connecticut's most popular figures because of his good sense, fairness, and willingness to listen to others and keep an open mind.

When the troubles with England began, Sherman hoped to avoid war. But while serving in the First Continental Congress, he was one of the first Americans to claim that the British Parliament didn't have the right to make laws for the Thirteen Colonies. In the Second Continental Congress he was on the committees that drafted the Declaration of Independence and the early national laws called the Articles of Confederation.

Roger Sherman's greatest service to his country came in 1787, when he helped create the U. S. Constitution, which replaced the Articles of Confederation. Except for Benjamin Franklin of Pennsylvania, he was the oldest member of the Constitutional Convention. And except for Gouverneur Morris and James Wilson of Pennsylvania and James Madison of Virginia, Sherman made the most speeches at the convention.

Sherman solved a big problem concerning the number of senators and representatives each state would have in the national government. Thanks to Sherman's Connecticut Compromise, it was decided that each state would have two senators, but its number of representatives would be based on population. This system has served the nation well for over 200 years.

Roger Sherman helped the Constitution get approved in Connecticut, and in his last years he served in the U. S. House of Representatives and then in the Senate. Roger Sherman, who had fifteen children with his two wives, died at the age of seventy-two in his home in New Haven, Connecticut. He was the only person to sign all of four key documents in early U. S. history: the Articles of Association in 1774; the Declaration of Independence in 1776; the Articles of Confederation in 1777; and the U. S. Constitution in 1787.

# Colonial America Time Line

Before the arrival of Europeans, many millions of Indians belonging to dozens of tribes lived in North America (and also in Central and South America)

**About 982 A.D.**—Eric the Red, born in Norway, reaches Greenland during one of the first European voyages to North America

**About 985**—Eric the Red brings settlers from Iceland to Greenland

**About 1000**—Leif Ericson (Eric the Red's son) leads what is thought to be the first European expedition to mainland North America; Leif probably lands in Canada

**1492**—Christopher Columbus, sailing for Spain, reaches America

**1497**—John Cabot reaches Canada in the first English voyage to North America

**1513**—Ponce de León of Spain explores Florida

**1519-1521**—Hernando Cortés of Spain conquers Mexico

**1565**—St. Augustine, Florida, the first permanent European town in what is now the United States, is founded by the Spanish

**1607**—Jamestown, Virginia, is founded, the first permanent English town in the present-day United States

**1608**—Frenchman Samuel de Champlain founds the village of Quebec, Canada

**1609**—Henry Hudson explores the eastern coast of present-day United States for The Netherlands; the Dutch then claim parts of New York, New Jersey, Delaware, and Connecticut and name the area New Netherland

**1619**—Virginia's House of Burgesses, America's first representative lawmaking body, is founded

**1619**—The first shipment of black slaves arrives in Jamestown

**1620**—English Pilgrims found Massachusetts' first permanent town at Plymouth

**1621**—Massachusetts Pilgrims and Indians hold the famous first Thanksgiving feast in colonial America

**1622**—Indians kill 347 settlers in Virginia

**1623**—Colonization of New Hampshire is begun by the English

**1624**—Colonization of present-day New York State is begun by the Dutch at Fort Orange (Albany)

**1625**—The Dutch start building New Amsterdam (now New York City)

**1630**—The town of Boston, Massachusetts, is founded by the English Puritans

**1633**—Colonization of Connecticut is begun by the English

**1634**—Colonization of Maryland is begun by the English

**1635**—Boston Latin School, the colonies' first public school, is founded

**1636**—Harvard, the colonies' first college, is founded in Massachusetts

**1636**—Rhode Island colonization begins when Englishman Roger Williams founds Providence

**1638**—The colonies' first library is established at Harvard

**1638**—Delaware colonization begins when Swedish people build Fort Christina at present-day Wilmington

**1640**—Stephen Daye of Cambridge, Massachusetts, prints *The Bay Psalm Book*, the first English-language book published in what is now the United States

**1643**—Swedish settlers begin colonizing Pennsylvania

**1647**—Massachusetts forms the first public school system in the colonies

**1650**—North Carolina is colonized by Virginia settlers in about this year

**1650**—Population of colonial United States is about 50,000

**1660**—New Jersey colonization is begun by the Dutch at present-day Jersey City

**1670**—South Carolina colonization is begun by the English near Charleston

**1673**—Jacques Marquette and Louis Jolliet explore the upper Mississippi River for France

**1675-76**—New England colonists beat Indians in King Philip's War

**1682**—Philadelphia, Pennsylvania, is settled

**1682**—La Salle explores Mississippi River all the way to its mouth in Louisiana and claims the whole Mississippi Valley for France

**1693**—College of William and Mary is founded in Williamsburg, Virginia

**1700**—Colonial population is about 250,000

**1704**—*The Boston News-Letter*, the first successful newspaper in the colonies, is founded

**1706**—Benjamin Franklin is born in Boston

**1732**—George Washington, future first president of the United States, is born in Virginia

**1733**—English begin colonizing Georgia, their thirteenth colony in what is now the United States

**1735**—John Adams, future second president, is born in Massachusetts

**1743**—Thomas Jefferson, future third president, is born in Virginia

**1750**—Colonial population is about 1,200,000

**1754**—France and England begin fighting the French and Indian War over North American lands

**1763**—England, victorious in the war, gains Canada and most other French lands east of the Mississippi River

**1764**—British pass Sugar Act to gain tax money from the colonists

**1765**—British pass the Stamp Act, which the colonists despise; colonists then hold the Stamp Act Congress in New York City

**1766**—British repeal the Stamp Act

**1770**—British soldiers kill five Americans in the "Boston Massacre"

**1773**—Colonists dump British tea into Boston Harbor at the "Boston Tea Party"

**1774**—British close up port of Boston to punish the city for the tea party

**1774**—Delegates from all the colonies but Georgia meet in Philadelphia at the First Continental Congress

**1775**—**April 19:** Revolutionary War begins at Lexington and Concord, Massachusetts

      **May 10:** Second Continental Congress convenes in Philadelphia

      **June 17:** Colonists inflict heavy losses on British but lose Battle of Bunker Hill near Boston

      **July 3:** George Washington takes command of Continental Army

**1776**—**March 17:** Washington's troops force the British out of Boston in the first major American victory of the war

      **May 4:** Rhode Island is first colony to declare itself independent of Britain

**July 4:** Declaration of Independence is adopted

**December 26:** Washington's forces win Battle of Trenton (New Jersey)

1777—**January 3:** Americans win at Princeton, New Jersey

**August 16:** Americans win Battle of Bennington at New York-Vermont border

**September 11:** British win Battle of Brandywine Creek near Philadelphia

**September 26:** British capture Philadelphia

**October 4:** British win Battle of Germantown near Philadelphia

**October 17:** About 5,000 British troops surrender at Battle of Saratoga in New York

**December 19:** American army goes into winter quarters at Valley Forge, Pennsylvania, where more than 3,000 soldiers die by spring

1778—**February 6:** France joins the American side

**July 4:** American George Rogers Clark captures Kaskaskia, Illinois, from the British

1779—**February 23-25:** George Rogers Clark captures Vincennes in Indiana

**September 23:** American John Paul Jones captures British ship *Serapis*

1780—**May 12:** British take Charleston, South Carolina

**August 16:** British badly defeat Americans at Camden, South Carolina

**October 7:** Americans defeat British at Kings Mountain, South Carolina

1781—**January 17:** Americans win battle at Cowpens, South Carolina

**March 1:** Articles of Confederation go into effect as laws of the United States

**March 15:** British suffer heavy losses at Battle of Guilford Courthouse in North Carolina; British then give up most of North Carolina

**October 19:** British army under Charles Cornwallis surrenders at Yorktown, Virginia, as major Revolutionary War fighting ends

1783—**September 3:** United States officially wins Revolution as the United States and Great Britain sign Treaty of Paris

**November 25:** Last British troops leave New York City

1787—On December 7, Delaware becomes the first state by approving the U.S. Constitution

1788—On June 21, New Hampshire becomes the ninth state when it approves the U.S. Constitution; with nine states having approved it, the Constitution goes into effect as the law of the United States

1789—On April 30, George Washington is inaugurated as first president of the United States

1790—On May 29, Rhode Island becomes the last of the original thirteen colonies to become a state

1791—U.S. Bill of Rights goes into effect on December 15

## About the Author

Dennis Brindell Fradin is the author of more than 100 published children's books. His works for Childrens Press include the Young People's Stories of Our States series, the Disaster! series, and the Thirteen Colonies series. His other books are *Remarkable Children* (Little, Brown), which is about twenty children who made history, and a science-fiction novel entitled *How I Saved the World* (Dillon). Dennis is married to Judith Bloom Fradin, a high-school English teacher. They have two sons named Tony and Mike and a daughter named Diana Judith. Dennis was graduated from Northwestern University in 1967 with a B.A. in creative writing, and has lived in Evanston, Illinois, since that year.

## Photo Credits